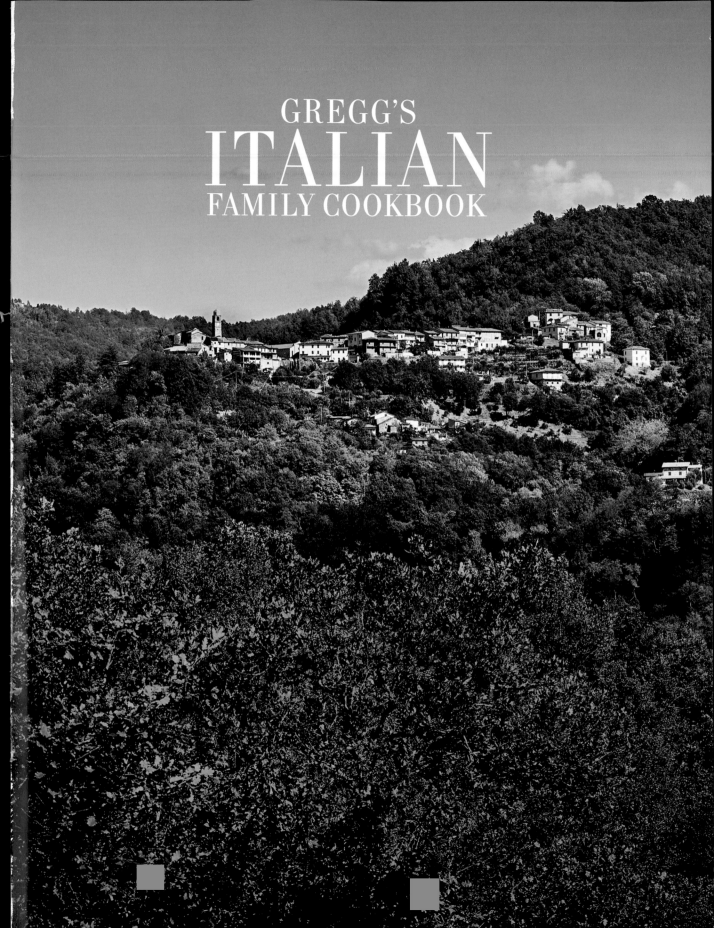

GREGG'S
ITALIAN
FAMILY COOKBOOK

Dedicated to the strength that comes from family. *Bella Familia.*

GREGG'S ITALIAN FAMILY COOKBOOK

Gregg & Anna Wallace

MITCHELL BEAZLEY

INTRODUCTION

I fell in love with the foods of Italy on my first-ever visit to the country over 20 years ago. Since then, I have been fortunate enough to visit Italy at least once every year, and my love has never wavered. In my opinion, the stunning flavours and beautiful simplicity of the dishes make Italian cuisine the best in the world, and it must surely be one of the country's most successful exports. I can't think of anywhere nowadays that you can't get a bowl of pasta or a slice of pizza. In fact, if the Neapolitans had copyrighted the pizza, they would now be fabulously wealthy.

Over time, I've become aware that there really isn't any such thing as "Italian food". Instead, there are lots of regional foods under the Italian umbrella, and that's why I refer to "the foods of Italy" rather than "Italian food". Every region has its own particular style and flavours. Think of Apulia with its orecchiette (little ears) pasta, Calabria and its liberal use of chillies, Campania with its legendary pizza, Tuscany with its stunning beef, Lombardy with its creamy risottos, Piedmont and its truffles, Liguria with its *pesce crudo* (raw fish) and, of course, Emilia-Romagna with Parma ham and Parmesan cheese.

It was a happy accident that I met and fell in love with an Italian woman. I have to confess, it wasn't just her beauty and personality I fell for; it was also her passion for feasting and cooking. Our trips away always seem to centre around a *grande pranzo* (big lunch), and we have shared many wonderful Italian food experiences. Every August we rent a house for a month somewhere in Italy, drive down with our favourite cooking utensils, invite the family and hide away from anyone who might recognize us. While there, we cook and cook and cook. We also sip the odd glass of wine.

Although I've loved the food of Italy for a long time, marrying into an Italian family has increased my knowledge and heightened my appreciation for it. Mealtimes have become so much more than they ever used to be. Anna is a fabulous cook, just like her mamma and papa, Rina and Massimo, and they've all taught me a lot. Mostly what I've learned is that flavour is everything, and every meal, no matter how simple, is best savoured slowly. It's about bringing the family together, enjoying big glasses of wine and getting splashes of tomato sauce on your napkin.

The recipes in this book aren't difficult – the food of Italy rarely is. Over the course of these pages, Anna and I, Rina, Massimo and Anna's nonna share the stories and memories of our favourite dishes, showing that these recipes come from an Italian family with a love of food, laughter and each other. What we want to do is pass on our joy of cooking and eating to you because the best food you'll ever eat is in the home. Get the family involved, tuck in your napkin, slurp your spaghetti, enjoy another glass of wine, play some opera and, above all, enjoy!

Here are some of my favourite snaps of the people who have taught me the most about the love of food – my Dad (Massimo), my Mum (Rina) and my Nonna. *Anna*

Nonna

Massimo

Me

Rina

My love of food started when I was about six years old and being looked after by my Roman nonna (grandmother) while my parents worked. I have many wonderful memories from that time, but the summers are particularly vivid because we were so often in the garden picking fresh peaches, big bright lemons, juicy red tomatoes and lovely salad greens, all of which we took back to the kitchen to cook.

I liked to get messy while helping Nonna to make pasta dough, and would watch for hours while she rolled it out and made a tomato sauce.

Shopping was also an adventure. We would go to colourful markets and tiny shops to buy whatever couldn't be produced at home. Even now, I remember visiting the local butcher for steaks, and I can still recall the sizzle as they hit the pan and filled the kitchen with a rich and delicious smell. Is it any wonder that with these formative experiences, I have always loved to cook?

I am very proud of my Italian heritage. From an early age I visited Italy every year with my parents, and I remember enjoying many happy family feasts outside my uncle's house in the mountains. We would sit for hours at a long table laden with delicious food all made with produce from my uncle's land, and be laughing, eating and talking from midday until the sun was setting.

Food has always been a large part of my life, and of course it's a huge part of Gregg's life too. We have a shared passion for Italy and we visit as often as we can. We both love the fact that Italian food is rustic and simple – no fancy foams, towers or squiggles – it is just what it is. For example, take a few good, simple ingredients, such as ripe tomatoes, basil, olive oil, salt and bread, and you can quickly make delicious bruschette – an authentic taste of Italy in just a few minutes.

To my mind, food is about far more than feeding our bodies – it is about creating, experimenting and relaxing, a way of being together, sharing experiences and making memories. I love how food can take you back to a certain place or time, conjuring up your childhood, a holiday or a love affair.

It makes me happy to cook and to make other people around me happy with what I have created. I can always tell when something is going down well because all I hear are appreciative sounds, "Mmmm, yum" and "Is there any more?" That always brings a smile to my face.

I believe this book will allow you to create great food for any occasion, whether it's a family meal, a quick snack, a big bowl of comfort food, a romantic dinner for two, or a celebration. I hope it becomes a constant source of ideas in your kitchen, loved enough to be spotted with tomato sauce and floury fingerprints!

Chapter One

ANTIPASTI

INSALATA DI MOZZARELLA E POMODORO

SERVES 4

4 x 150g (5½oz) buffalo
mozzarella cheese,
drained
600g (1lb 5oz) tomatoes
(any mixture you like)
2 tablespoons olive oil,
for drizzling
Salt and freshly ground
black pepper
Large handful of fresh
basil leaves, to serve

As a child, I always spent the summer with my nonna in Italy. We would visit the local buffalo mozzarella shop every day, and I can clearly remember walking into the chilled room through the beaded curtains across the door. The mozzarella would be placed in a clear plastic bag filled with salted water, and I couldn't wait to get home and eat it. The cheese had many layers to it, and I would sit and peel them off until I reached the delectable creamy centre. Fresh mozzarella, combined with sweet red tomatoes and fresh basil, makes a simple and beautiful salad. *Anna*

Tear your mozzarella into pieces – there's something very satisfying about this and it gives the salad a lovely rustic look, but you can use a knife if you prefer. Place on a large serving plate.

Chop the tomatoes into chunks and scatter them over the mozzarella. Drizzle with the olive oil and season with salt and pepper. Tear the basil into pieces and scatter over the salad.

Yes, it's really that easy!

OCTOPUS SALAD

INSALATA DI POLPO

SERVES 4

5 cooked and frozen
octopus tentacles,
defrosted (available
from online
fishmongers)
100ml (3½fl oz)
olive oil
Juice of 1½ lemons
4 tablespoons chopped
flat leaf parsley
1 red chilli, deseeded
and finely chopped,
or ½ teaspoon dried
chilli flakes
½ teaspoon salt

I love octopus. As a young boy growing up in Esperia, part
of Lazio, the region that includes Rome, I spent many
summers with one of my relatives who had a beach hut.
We regularly went out on fishing boats to see what we could
catch, and octopus was one of my favourites. I love its sweet,
meaty flesh, which is great simply boiled, then chopped up
in a salad. One of the tips I learned, and that I still use today,
is to boil octopus with corks: the natural enzyme cork
contains tenderizes the flesh. *Massimo*

Cut the tentacles into 2.5cm (1 inch) pieces and place
in a bowl.

Combine all the remaining ingredients in a separate
bowl and stir well. Pour this dressing over the octopus
and leave to stand for 30 minutes before serving, so that
the flavours develop.

INSALATA ANTIPASTO

SERVES 4–6

160g (5¾oz) pitted
 green olives
160g (5¾oz) artichokes
 in oil, drained
200g (7oz) provolone
 cheese, cut into cubes
150g (5½oz) chunk of
 salami, cut into cubes
250g (9oz) mini
 mozzarella cheeses
Large handful of fresh
 basil leaves, to serve

For the dressing
6 tablespoons olive oil
3 tablespoons red
 wine vinegar
1 teaspoon sugar
1 teaspoon dried oregano

I have very fond memories of big family meals at my uncle's lovely home in the mountains. This delicious salad was always served, and gave a fantastic splash of colour to the table. *Anna*

First make the dressing by combining the ingredients for it in a bowl and stirring well.

Combine all the remaining ingredients, apart from the basil, in a salad bowl. Pour the dressing over them and toss well.

Tear the basil leaves over your salad. Serve with crusty bread.

PANZANELLA

SERVES 4–6

650g (1lb 7oz) day-old
    ciabatta or sourdough
    bread
6 fairly large tomatoes,
    chopped into chunks
1 shallot, diced
100ml (3½fl oz) extra
    virgin olive oil
4 teaspoons red or white
    wine vinegar
1 teaspoon salt
Large handful of fresh
    basil leaves, to serve

My mother hated to throw anything away, and I think that's because people of her generation in Italy had lived through tough times. Bread going hard would be used to make this lovely salad. *Rina*

Lightly wet the bread under your cold water tap so that it is moistened all the way through. If it's too wet, gently squeeze out the excess water. You don't want it to turn into clumps.

Tear the bread into a large salad bowl. You can keep some of the pieces quite large, but the bread can be crumbled if you would prefer it to look like breadcrumbs.

Add the tomatoes and shallot, and mix well with your hands. Pour in the olive oil and vinegar, add the salt and mix again.

To finish, tear the fresh basil and scatter it over the salad. The smell will be amazing!

You can eat the salad straight away, but if left at room temperature for about an hour (before you scatter over the basil), the bread will soak up all the lovely tomato juices.

FUNGHI ARANCINI

MAKES 15

100g (3½oz) plain flour
2 eggs, beaten
175g (6oz) breadcrumbs
100g (3½oz) Parmesan
   cheese, grated
850g (1lb 14oz) leftover
   mushroom risotto,
   cooled (see page 110)
200g (7oz) mozzarella
   cheese, cut into cubes
Sunflower oil,
   for deep-frying
Salt

These deep-fried balls of cheese-stuffed rice are a Sicilian favourite. If, like me, you always seem to cook too much risotto, you can turn the leftovers into these delicious mouthfuls. We use leftover mushroom risotto here, but the recipe works well with any type. *Anna*

Put the flour, eggs and breadcrumbs into 3 separate shallow bowls. Stir the Parmesan into the breadcrumbs.

Take a small handful of the risotto and shape it into a ball. Using your finger, make a small dent in the middle, insert a cube of mozzarella, then cover it with the rice and re-form it into a ball. You might need to add a little more rice to enclose the filling completely. Repeat this step until you have 15 balls.

Roll each ball first in the flour, then in the egg and finally in the breadcrumbs, making sure they are coated. Place on a plate.

Half-fill a large saucepan with oil and place over a medium heat until it reaches 180°C (350°F), or a cube of bread added to the oil browns within 30 seconds. When ready, gently lower the risotto balls, 2 or 3 at a time, into the hot oil and fry until golden brown all over. This should take about 3 minutes.

Using a slotted spoon, transfer them to a plate lined with kitchen paper and keep warm while you make the rest.

Season the arancini with salt, and then serve with a dip of your choice – spicy tomato ketchup (see page 41) or a chilli dip would work well.

FAVE CON PARMIGIANO E PANCETTA

SERVES 4

650g (1lb 7oz) fresh or
   frozen broad beans
Olive oil, for frying
130g (4½oz) smoked
   pancetta cubes
1 shallot, finely diced
Parmesan cheese,
   to serve

At our family home in southern Italy, my nonna would take me out into the garden, which was filled with many wonderful things to eat. There we would pick furry pods of broad beans, which I enjoyed splitting to get at the tender beans inside. This is my favourite way of cooking them – so simple yet so delicious. *Anna*

Cook the broad beans in a large pan of salted boiling water – 2 minutes for fresh beans and 4 minutes for frozen – then drain and set aside for about 10 minutes. When cool enough to handle, slip the beans out of their tough skins and tumble them into a bowl.

Warm a glug of olive oil in a frying pan over a medium-high heat. When hot, add the pancetta cubes and fry until golden, about 5 minutes, stirring occasionally. Add the shallot and fry for a few minutes, until softened.

Add the pancetta mixture to the broad beans and give them a good stir.

Using a vegetable peeler, shave the Parmesan over the top of the dish. That's it!

CARCIOFI FRITTI

SERVES 4

2 lemons
12 baby artichokes
Sunflower oil,
   for deep-frying
Salt

We were on holiday in Rome when we first tried these delightful little mouthfuls. As often happens, we'd found a great little eatery in one of the narrow backstreets and enjoyed these artichokes as part of a long, long lunch. We now cook them at home. *Anna & Gregg*

Fill a bowl with cold water and add the juice of 1 lemon. You will need this liquid to prevent the artichokes discolouring.

To prepare the artichokes, start by pulling off and discarding the tough outer leaves. Cut the top 1cm (½ inch) off the remaining leaves. Trim the bottom of the artichoke stem, then cut off the top outer layer of the stem. Place in the bowl of acidulated water.

Half-fill a large saucepan with oil and heat until it reaches 180°C (350°F), or a cube of bread added to the oil browns within 30 seconds. When ready, drain the artichokes and dry them thoroughly with kitchen paper. Gently add the artichokes to the pan a few at a time and fry until tender – about 10 minutes. Using a slotted spoon, transfer them to a plate lined with kitchen paper. Keep the oil on the heat.

Using the back of a large spoon, gently press each artichoke to flatten it out so that it looks like a flower.

Carefully lower the flattened artichokes into the oil and fry for a second time, until golden brown and crisp – about 1–2 minutes. Transfer to a plate freshly lined with kitchen paper and allow to drain for a few moments.

Transfer the artichokes to a serving plate, sprinkle with salt to taste and squeeze the remaining lemon over them. Eat straight away.

FIORI DI ZUCCA FRITTI

SERVES 4

100g (3½oz) plain flour
300ml (10fl oz)
    sparkling water
Sunflower oil,
    for deep-frying
12 courgette flowers,
    stamens removed
Salt

My mother grew courgettes in our garden, and I've always loved their flowers – they are so delicate and pretty. She would actually sell them in the market, but occasionally as a treat she would fry some for me. *Nonna*

Place the flour in a bowl and gradually whisk in the sparkling water to make a smooth batter. Season with salt.

Half-fill a large saucepan with oil and heat until it reaches 180°C (350°F), or a cube of bread added to the oil browns within 30 seconds. When ready, gently dip a courgette flower into the batter to coat completely, then lower it into the hot oil. Add another 1 or 2 flowers in the same way – don't overcrowd the pan – and fry for 3 minutes, or until golden brown.

Using a slotted spoon, transfer the cooked courgette flowers to a plate lined with kitchen paper. Cook the remaining flowers in the same way. Season with salt and serve straight away or they will become soggy.

OLIVE FRITTE RIPIENE

SERVES 4

40 large pitted
   green olives
4 tablespoons plain flour
3 eggs, beaten
200g (7oz) breadcrumbs
Sunflower oil, for
   deep-frying

For the stuffing
20 canned anchovies,
   cut into 15mm
   (⅝ inch) pieces
4 slices of Parma ham,
   each slice torn into
   about 10 pieces

We were out one day and, as often happens, stopped for a drink. Our order came with a bowl of these olives, so we stayed and had another drink and got another bowl. We now make them at home. *Massimo & Gregg*

Place the olives in a bowl, and place an empty bowl of similar size alongside it. Take one olive at a time and stuff a small piece of anchovy and a small piece of Parma ham into the cavity. Put the stuffed olive into the empty bowl and prepare the remaining olives in the same way.

Place the flour, eggs and breadcrumbs in 3 separate shallow bowls. Roll the olives in the flour, then the egg and finally the breadcrumbs. Repeat this step twice more so that the olives are well coated.

Half-fill a deep saucepan with oil and heat until it reaches 180°C (350°F), or a cube of bread added to the oil browns within 30 seconds. When ready, fry the olives in small batches until golden and crisp; they don't take long, so keep an eye on them. Using a slotted spoon, transfer the olives to a plate lined with kitchen paper.

Serve the olives with spicy tomato ketchup (see page 41) and a glass of cold beer or wine.

ROASTED PEPPERS

PEPERONI ARROSTITI

SERVES 4

2 large red peppers
2 large yellow peppers
5 tablespoons extra
  virgin olive oil
1–2 garlic cloves,
  crushed
3 canned anchovies
  (optional)
½ teaspoon salt (optional
  – use only if *not* using
  the anchovies)

Having been a greengrocer, I find it difficult to walk past an Italian shop of *frutta* and *vedura* without taking a good look. Peppers tend to be huge, elongated and irregular: the colours are like sunshine on a plate. *Gregg*

Preheat the oven to 220°C, 200°C fan (425°F), Gas Mark 7.

Place the peppers on their side on a baking sheet and drizzle with the olive oil. Roast for 45–60 minutes, turning them halfway through, until the skin is blackened and blistered.

Transfer the peppers to a plastic bag, seal tightly and let them sit in their own steam for 10–15 minutes. This will loosen the skin.

Remove the peppers and peel off the skin (this is quite messy!). Cut the peppers in half, remove the stalk and seeds and cut the flesh into strips. Transfer to a large flat plate.

Pound the garlic and anchovies or salt in a mortar until you have a paste. If you don't have a mortar, simply chop everything very finely on a board.

Spoon this mixture over your sunshine peppers, cover with clingfilm and place in the refrigerator. The longer you leave them (hard, I know), the tastier they become: at least 5 hours, but ideally overnight.

Serve at room temperature with crusty bread.

PATATINE DI POLENTA CON KETCHUP DI POMODORO PICCANTE

SERVES 6–9

375g (13oz) instant
  polenta
300ml (10fl oz)
  double cream
200g (7oz) Parmesan
  cheese, grated
100g (3½oz) fine
  cornmeal
Sunflower oil,
  for deep-frying

*For the spicy tomato
  ketchup*
1 x 200g (7oz) tube
  tomato purée
70g (2½oz) light
  brown sugar
4 tablespoons white
  wine vinegar
2 tablespoons water
1 teaspoon garlic powder
1 teaspoon salt, plus
  extra for sprinkling
2 teaspoons dried
  chilli flakes

One summer, I visited my great-aunt and -uncle in Castelforte, a picturesque town in central Italy. My great-aunt had a huge pot of bubbling polenta on the stove, which she kept stirring for a very long time. Eventually, the contents of the pot were emptied onto a long wooden board, and a rich tomato ragù was poured over the top. We devoured every bit. During that same stay, my great-aunt also showed me how to make polenta chips. *Anna*

Cook the polenta according to the packet instructions. Remove from the heat and stir in the cream and Parmesan.

Line a shallow baking tray with clingfilm, pour in your polenta and smooth with a spatula. Leave to cool slightly, then cover with clingfilm and refrigerate for at least 4 hours. You need the polenta to be firm or it will fall apart when fried.

Turn the chilled polenta onto a chopping board, discarding the clingfilm. Cut the polenta into fat chips about 7 x 2cm (2¾ x ¾ inches).

Place the cornmeal in a shallow bowl. Gently toss the chips in it until they are fully coated. Shake off any excess.

Half-fill a large saucepan with oil and place over a medium heat until it reaches 180°C (350°F), or a piece of polenta added to the oil sizzles and rises to the surface in roughly 30 seconds. Fry the polenta chips in small batches and don't be tempted to move them around as they will break. In about 6 minutes they will start to float to the surface, and are ready once they are a golden brown. Using a slotted spoon, transfer them to a plate lined with kitchen paper. Sprinkle with salt.

For the ketchup, blitz the ingredients in a blender until smooth and glossy. Serve with the chips. Store any leftover ketchup in an airtight container in the refrigerator for up to 1 week.

VERDURE ALLA GRIGLIA

GRILLED VEGETABLES

SERVES 4

2 aubergines
3 courgettes
4 Portobello mushrooms
8 spring onions
Sunflower oil,
    for drizzling
Salt

In Italy, vegetables aren't seen as a side dish – they are as central to a meal as meat or fish, and rightly celebrated. This recipe is perfect for a summer barbecue. *Gregg*

Using a mandoline or a knife, cut the aubergines and courgettes lengthways into slices about 1cm (½ inch) thick.

Cut your mushrooms into slices 2cm (¾ inch) thick – this is thicker than usual because mushrooms shrink slightly during cooking.

Give your spring onions a haircut by trimming off their wavy roots and dark green bits, then use the back of a knife to press down and slightly flatten them.

Place all the veg on a large plate and drizzle with enough oil to coat them nicely.

Heat a griddle pan or barbecue until very hot (if cooking indoors, your kitchen will become rather smoky during this step, but please don't worry). If you don't have a griddle pan, a frying pan is OK, but you won't get nice chargrilled lines across your vegetables. Line a large plate with kitchen paper.

Place your aubergines in the griddle pan or on the barbecue and leave to cook for 2 minutes without moving them. After that, press them down with a fork to create the chargrilled lines. Flip them over and repeat the cooking and pressing. Transfer them to the paper-lined plate. Repeat this step to cook all the other vegetables.

Once everything is cooked, sprinkle with salt and enjoy.

FRIED SQUID

CALAMARI FRITTI

SERVES 4

Sunflower oil,
   for deep-frying
500g (1lb 2oz) squid,
   including tentacles
   (ask your fishmonger
   to clean it for you)
450g (1lb) plain flour
Salt and freshly ground
   black pepper
Lemon wedges, to serve

It was Massimo's mum who showed me how to prepare squid like this, and whenever I cook it for my family, I think of her. *Rina*

———————————————————————

Half-fill a large saucepan with oil and heat until it reaches 180°C (350°F), or a cube of bread added to the oil browns within 30 seconds. Line a baking sheet with a few layers of kitchen paper.

Cut the squid tubes into rings 1cm (½ inch) thick. Combine the flour and some salt in a large bowl. Take a handful of the squid rings at a time and roll them in the flour until well coated. Shake off any excess, then carefully lower them into the oil and fry until light golden brown, about 1 minute. Using a slotted spoon, transfer them to the lined baking sheet to drain. Flour and fry the remaining rings in the same way.

Toss the squid tentacles in the seasoned flour and lower them into the hot oil. Take care because they do like to spit and splutter. Fry for about 3 minutes, as they take a little bit longer than the rings to crisp up. Drain on the lined baking sheet.

Season the squid with salt and pepper, and serve with wedges of lemon.

ALICI SU PANE TOSTATO CON BURRO

SERVES 2

Sourdough bread,
  cut into slices 2.5cm
  (1 inch) thick
Unsalted butter,
  for spreading
1 x 50g (1¾oz) can
  or jar good-quality
  anchovies, drained
  if necessary

This is a special memory. Anna and I had only been dating for a few months when we made a very romantic trip to Portofino. Summer day, beautiful girl, glass of white wine and the simple delight of salty anchovies, melting butter and crispy toast. Italian perfection in every way. *Gregg*

Toast the bread, then spread with a thick layer of butter.

Lay 3 or 4 anchovies across the surface and scoff straight away.

GRILLED SARDINES

SARDE ALLA GRIGLIA

SERVES 4

20 fresh sardines,
    cleaned and scaled
    with heads left on
Olive oil, for drizzling
Salt and freshly ground
    black pepper
Lemon wedges, to serve

For the dressing
2 tablespoons olive oil
1 tablespoon white
    wine vinegar
1 garlic clove, very
    finely chopped
2 tablespoons
    chopped capers
3 tablespoons finely
    chopped flat leaf
    parsley
1 teaspoon salt

I have very fond memories of sardines. It was on a trip to Gaeta, a coastal city in central Italy, that my dad and I came across a fish market, where we bought some sardines. They looked metallic in the sunlight, but tasted wonderful when Dad cooked them on an improvised barbecue beside the sea. *Anna*

Soak 20 bamboo skewers in cold water for 30 minutes. This will prevent them from burning when the fish are cooked.

Preheat a grill or barbecue to a medium-high heat.

Meanwhile, pierce each sardine from head to tail with a skewer. Drizzle them with olive oil and season with salt and pepper. Place under the grill or on the barbecue and cook for 3 minutes on each side, or until cooked through.

While the fish are cooking, combine all the dressing ingredients in a jug and mix well.

Arrange the sardines on a large plate and pour the herby dressing all over them. Add the lemon wedges, then tuck in!

BEEF CARPACCIO

SERVES 4

1½ tablespoons
  fennel seeds
1 tablespoon mixed
  peppercorns
1 tablespoon Dijon
  mustard
1 garlic clove, grated
2 tablespoons olive oil,
  plus extra for drizzling
1 x 800g (1lb 12oz)
  beef fillet
Sunflower oil, for frying

When Gregg and I were on holiday in San Gimignano, a medieval hill town in Tuscany, we found a lovely little restaurant with beautiful views of green hills and trees. We sat al fresco and ordered some food to share, and one of dishes we got was wafer-thin slices of beef with black truffle shaved over the top. It was very good indeed and, along with a glass of vino rosso and a beautiful sunset, made us very happy. *Anna*

Place your fennel seeds in a dry frying pan over a medium-high heat and gently toast them for a few minutes to bring out their flavour. This will make your kitchen smell beautiful. Transfer the seeds to a mortar, add the peppercorns and grind to a powder.

Put the mustard, garlic and olive oil into a bowl and mix well.

Trim the ends and all the sinew from the beef, then smother the fillet in the mustard mixture and roll in the fragrant fennel and peppercorn dust. Wrap the beef in clingfilm and place in the refrigerator for 1 hour.

Pour a glug of sunflower oil into a frying pan and place over a high heat. When hot, sear the beef all over for about 2 minutes, until nicely browned. Wrap the fillet tightly in clingfilm to form a sausage: this will give you nice round slices when you come to carve it later on. Set aside until cool, then place in the refrigerator for at least 4 hours.

Before serving, unwrap the beef and use a very sharp knife to slice it as thinly as possible. If you want the slices to be even thinner, place them between 2 sheets of clingfilm and roll with a rolling pin.

Arrange the beef on a plate, drizzle with a little olive oil and serve.

CROSTINI CON GORGONZOLA E MASCARPONE

SERVES 4

1 ciabatta loaf
Olive oil, for brushing

*For the sugared
  walnuts (optional)*
100g (3½oz) walnut
  halves
50g (1¾oz) golden
  caster sugar
1 tablespoon butter

For the topping
175g (6oz) Gorgonzola
  cheese
100g (3½oz)
  mascarpone cheese
Salt

Crostini means "little crusts", and they make great antipasti when
served with delicious toppings. Everybody loves them. *Anna*

_____

Preheat the oven to 220°C, 200°C fan (425°F), Gas Mark 7.

Cut the bread diagonally into slices 5mm (¼ inch) thick.
Lightly brush both sides of the slices with olive oil and place
on a baking sheet. Place in the oven for 5 minutes, then flip
the crostini over and bake for another 5 minutes, or until they
turn golden brown. Set aside for 2 minutes to cool slightly.

If making the sugared walnuts, place a non-stick frying pan
over a medium heat. When hot, add the walnuts, sugar and
butter and heat for 5 minutes, stirring frequently with a
wooden spoon so the mixture doesn't catch and burn.

Line a baking sheet with baking parchment, tip the nut
mixture onto it and allow to harden; this should take about
10 minutes.

To make the topping, put the Gorgonzola into a bowl and
mash well with a fork until it's smooth and creamy. Add the
mascarpone, a pinch of salt and mix really well. It doesn't
matter if there are a few lumps – they won't affect the
flavour in any way.

To serve, place a spoonful of the lovely cheese mixture on
each crostini and spread it across the surface. Dot with
the sugared walnuts, if using.

TALEGGIO AL FORNO CON MIELE AL TARTUFO

SERVES 4

400g (14oz)
    Taleggio cheese
8 tablespoons
    truffle honey (plain
    honey may be used as
    an alternative)
4 sprigs of thyme
Salt and freshly ground
    black pepper

During a family holiday in Lazio, we went to a restaurant where we all loved this simple but brilliant starter. It's the only time I can remember us all ordering the same thing. *Gregg*

Preheat the oven to 200°C, 180°C fan (400°F), Gas Mark 6.

Divide the cheese into 4 equal pieces and place them in individual ovenproof dishes. Drizzle 2 tablespoons of the truffle honey over each serving and add a sprig of thyme. Season well with salt and pepper and bake for 10 minutes, or until gooey.

Enjoy with warm crusty bread.

BAGNA CAUDA

SERVES 4

6 garlic cloves, peeled
whole milk (just enough
   to cover the garlic in
   the pan)
90g (3¼oz) canned
   or jarred anchovies,
   drained if necessary
60g (2¼oz) unsalted
   butter
100ml (3½fl oz)
   extra virgin olive oil
100ml (3½fl oz)
   single cream
crudités, for dipping
   (e.g. baby gem lettuce
   leaves, carrots, celery,
   chicory, fennel, radishes,
   spring onions)

I first tasted this dip on *MasterChef*, and it was my mother-in-law Rina who showed me how to make it. She herself first tasted it on honeymoon at a party thrown by her new husband's sister. *Gregg*

Place the garlic in a heavy-based saucepan. Add just enough whole milk to cover the garlic and place over a low heat. Warm gently for 5 minutes.

Transfer the milk and garlic to a blender or food processor, add the anchovies, butter and olive oil and blend until smooth. Pour the mixture back into the saucepan and warm gently, stirring constantly, for about 2 minutes. When it thickens slightly, stir in the cream.

Pour the mixture into a dish and serve immediately, along with some crudités for dipping. *Delizioso*!

STUFFED MUSHROOMS

FUNGHI RIPIENI

SERVES 4

6 large Portobello
   mushrooms
4 slices of Parma ham
Olive oil, for frying and
   drizzling
3 shallots, finely chopped
2 garlic cloves, grated
175g (6oz) breadcrumbs
225g (8oz) Parmesan
   cheese, grated
100g (3½oz) flat leaf
   parsley, finely chopped
2 eggs, beaten
Salt and freshly ground
   black pepper

When I was younger, I spent a lot of time in my nonna's kitchen, and I learned so much, including how to stuff mushrooms. I did make quite a mess, but it was fun and I was really proud when I later made them for my mum and dad. They were very impressed by their 12-year-old daughter's achievement and devoured the lot. *Anna*

Preheat the oven to 220°C, 200°C fan (425°F), Gas Mark 7.

Remove the stalks from 4 of the mushrooms and reserve for later. Place a slice of Parma ham on each mushroom and set aside.

Take the remaining 2 mushrooms and the reserved stalks and finely chop them.

Pour a glug of oil into a frying pan and place over a medium heat. Add the shallots and chopped mushrooms and cook for about 5 minutes, until softened. Stir in the garlic and continue to cook for another minute. Set aside.

Place the breadcrumbs in a bowl and add all but 4 tablespoons of the Parmesan, the parsley and eggs, plus some salt and pepper. Mix really well.

Spoon mounds of the stuffing onto the ham-covered mushrooms, then sprinkle with the remaining Parmesan. Place on a baking sheet, drizzle with a little olive oil and bake for 30 minutes.

CARTA DI MUSICA

MAKES 4 SHEETS

130g (4½oz) "00" flour,
   plus extra for dusting
130g (4½oz) semolina
1 teaspoon salt, plus extra
   for sprinkling
200ml (7fl oz) water

The name of this bread stems from the fact that the uncooked dough is thin enough for a sheet of music to be read through it. Gregg and I like to think that the music comes from the way the bread "sings" when you crack it open. *Anna*

Preheat the oven to 240°C, 220°C fan (475°F), Gas Mark 9. Line 2 baking sheets with baking parchment.

Combine the flour, semolina and salt in a bowl and make a well in the centre. Pour in the water bit by bit, mixing constantly with a wooden spoon until a dough forms (you might not need all the water). Using your hands, shape the dough into a ball, then turn it onto a floured surface and knead for 15 minutes, until smooth and soft.

Cut the dough into 4 equal-sized pieces. Using a rolling pin, roll each piece out very thinly into an oblong shape. The thinner you roll it, the crispier your breads will be. Carefully place two pieces of rolled-out dough on the prepared sheets.

Bake for 4 minutes, until golden and puffed up. The breads may still be slightly soft when they come out of the oven, but will soon harden as they cool. Repeat with the remaining two pieces of dough.

Season with salt and enjoy with dips or on their own.

Note: On one occasion when I made these breads I had some dough left over, and found myself wondering if it could be cooked and used like pasta. To my surprise, it worked a treat. I simply boiled strips of it for 3 minutes, drained them and added a knob of butter and some Parmesan.

FOCACCIA

SERVES 8

For the starter
300g (10½oz) strong
    white bread flour
1 teaspoon dried yeast
300ml (10fl oz) water

For the dough
3 teaspoons dried yeast
200ml (7fl oz) warm water
500g (1lb 2oz) strong
    white bread flour, plus
    extra for dusting
80ml (2¾fl oz) olive oil
15g (½oz) salt

For the topping
1 tablespoon olive oil,
    plus extra for drizzling
2 tablespoons freshly
    chopped rosemary
    leaves
1 tablespoon water
Salt

When I was a little girl, my mother would bake this bread in an outdoor oven, and I can still recall the wonderful smells of yeast and rosemary. *Nonna*

With this loaf, you need to make a starter dough the day before you intend to bake. Place the flour, yeast and water in a large bowl and mix well. Cover and leave in a warm place overnight.

The following day, make the dough. Put the yeast and warm water into a bowl, mix well, then set aside. The yeast will start to activate.

Put the flour into a large bowl, add the olive oil and salt, then mix in the activated yeast. Add this dough to your starter dough and mix thoroughly by hand.

Tip the dough onto a floured work surface and knead for 10–15 minutes, pushing and stretching the dough away from you, then rolling it back on itself toward you. Transfer to a lightly oiled bowl, then cover and leave to rise in a warm place for 4 hours, or until the dough has doubled in size.

Place the dough on the work surface again and roll it into an oblong shape. Don't worry if it's not perfectly regular.

Oil a baking tray about 24 x 18 cm (9½ x 7 inches). Sit the dough in it, then stretch and press it out to fill the entire tray. Using your fingertips, make dents in the surface. Cover with a cloth and set aside again in a warm place for 1 hour.

Preheat the oven to 220°C, 200°C fan (425°F), Gas Mark 7.

Top the dough with the olive oil and rosemary, then sprinkle with the water (this creates a crisp surface) and a generous sprinkling of salt.

Bake for 20 minutes, until golden brown and the bread sounds hollow when tapped on the bottom. Drizzle some extra olive oil over the top, then allow to cool before serving.

BRUSCHETTE

SERVES 4

1 sourdough or ciabatta
   loaf, cut into slices
   2cm (¾ inch) thick
2 tablespoons extra
   virgin olive oil
1 garlic clove, cut in half

Tomato and basil topping
500g (1lb 2oz) baby
   plum tomatoes
Olive oil, for drizzling
Large handful of basil
   leaves
Salt

Mushroom topping
1 tablespoon olive oil
1 garlic clove, grated
600g (1lb 5oz) mixed
   mushrooms, chopped
2 tablespoons chopped
   flat leaf parsley
Salt and freshly ground
   black pepper

*Cannellini bean and
   truffle oil topping*
Olive oil, for frying
1 garlic clove, crushed
2 x 500g (1lb 2oz) cans
   cannellini beans,
   rinsed and drained
Salt and freshly ground
   black pepper
White or black truffle oil
   (olive oil may be used as
   an alternative), to serve

My niece's wedding feast in Monte Cassino went on for the whole day, with course after course of tasty food. It's a family tradition that all the family help to prepare the food for a wedding, so Rina and I helped to make the trays and trays of bruschette that greeted the guests along with a glass of vino. Bruschette are very versatile, and can be topped with whatever you like. My favourite toppings are below. *Massimo*

Preheat oven to 220°C, 200°C fan (425°F), Gas Mark 7. Place the slices of bread on a baking sheet. Drizzle them with olive oil on both sides and toast for 2 minutes on each side. Set aside to cool.

To make the tomato and basil topping, chop the tomatoes into small pieces. Place in a bowl, drizzle with olive oil and add a pinch of salt. Tear the basil leaves (using a knife makes them bruise and discolour) and add them to the bowl.

With a spoon, slightly crush the tomatoes so that they release some of their juices. You could leave the tomatoes for 1 hour so that the flavours intensify, but you don't have to. Rub one side of each piece of toast with the garlic, then spoon the vivid tomato mixture on top. Serve straight away.

To make the mushroom topping, put the olive oil into a frying pan over a high heat. When hot, add the garlic and fry for 20 seconds, then add the mushrooms and fry until they are soft. Season with salt and pepper, then add the parsley and give it a good stir. Spoon the garlicky mushroom mixture on top of the bruschette. Serve straight away.

To make the cannellini bean and truffle oil topping, heat a glug of olive oil in a saucepan, then add the garlic and cook for 1 minute, stirring occasionally. Tumble in your cannellini beans, season with salt and pepper and cook for 5–8 minutes. Using a fork or potato masher, gently mash the beans to create a creamy but chunky texture. Spoon the bean mixture onto the bruschette, then drizzle with truffle oil. Serve straight away.

Chapter Two

FIRST COURSES

ZUPPA DI FAGIOLI BIANCHI E AGLIO

SERVES 4

125ml (4fl oz) extra
 virgin olive oil
1 garlic clove,
 finely chopped
2 x 400g cans cannellini
 beans, rinsed and
 drained
250ml (9fl oz)
 vegetable stock
4 thick slices of
 white bread
2 tablespoons chopped
 flat leaf parsley
Salt and freshly ground
 black pepper

When I was a schoolboy, I would often get home to find this soup bubbling away in a cast iron pot over an open fire. It was so welcoming and satisfying that I still think of it fondly. *Massimo*

Put the olive oil into a saucepan over a medium heat and fry the garlic, stirring often, until it turns a light golden colour. Be careful not to let it overbrown or the flavour will be bitter.

Tumble in the beans, add the stock, a pinch of salt and a few twists of pepper, then cover and simmer gently for 5 minutes.

Spoon roughly half the beans into a blender, add just a little of the stock and blitz until you have a purée. Don't worry if it's not completely smooth – the more rustic the better.

Return the purée to the pan of beans, stir well, then cover and simmer for another 6 minutes.

While the soup is simmering away, toast the bread and place each slice in an individual soup bowl.

Sprinkle the parsley into the soup, and turn off the heat.

Ladle the soup over the toast and serve straight away.

Molto saporito!

MINESTRONE

SERVES 4–6

3 tablespoons olive oil
200g (7oz) bacon lardons
1 large onion, diced
3 carrots, diced
3 celery sticks, diced
1 tablespoon tomato purée
1 Parmesan rind (optional)
½ head of Savoy cabbage,
   chopped
1 garlic clove, crushed
1 teaspoon dried oregano
2 tablespoons finely
   chopped flat leaf
   parsley
1 x 400g (14oz) can
   chopped tomatoes
750ml (27fl oz) vegetable
   stock
100g (3½oz) ditalini
   pasta or small
   pasta tubes
2 x 400g (14oz) cans
   cannellini beans,
   rinsed and drained
Salt and freshly ground
   black pepper
100g (3½oz) Parmesan
   cheese, grated, to serve

A colourful and hearty soup, this tastes even better 24 hours after it's been made, so why not double up the amounts and have it over a few days? It contains tons of veg, so is really good for you. *Gregg*

Put the olive oil into a large pan over a medium heat. When hot, add the bacon lardons and fry for 1 minute, then add the onion, carrots, celery, tomato purée, Parmesan rind (if using) and a pinch of salt and pepper. Cook, stirring often, for about 5 minutes, until the vegetables have softened.

Add the cabbage, garlic, oregano and parsley. Cook for 6 minutes.

Pour in the tomatoes and stock, bring to a gentle simmer, then partially cover the pan with a lid. Cook for 2 hours, stirring occasionally.

Meanwhile, cook the pasta according to the packet instructions, then drain and set aside.

When the 2 hours are up, add the cooked pasta and the cannellini beans. Cook for a further 30 minutes.

Ladle the soup into deep bowls, sprinkle with the Parmesan and tuck in.

RIBOLLITA

SERVES 4

4 tablespoons extra virgin
   olive oil, plus extra for
   drizzling
130g (4½oz) smoked
   pancetta cubes
1 large leek, chopped
2 carrots, roughly chopped
3 celery sticks
1 small head of Savoy
   cabbage, shredded
2 garlic cloves, 1 crushed
   and 1 cut in half
1 x 400g (14oz) can
   chopped tomatoes
1 tablespoon tomato purée
1 x 400g (14oz) can
   cannellini beans,
   rinsed and drained
300ml (10fl oz) chicken
   stock
1 Parmesan rind
4 ciabatta rolls, sliced in
   half, or 4 thick slices
   of sourdough bread
Salt and freshly ground
   black pepper

To serve
Freshly grated Parmesan
   cheese
Handful of flat leaf
   parsley, roughly
   chopped

This is a dish that we had a lot during the war. It was a great way of using up any leftover bread and vegetables, but was also very comforting and nutritious. Of course, it tastes just as good nowadays. *Nonna*

Put the olive oil into a large saucepan over a medium heat. When hot, add the pancetta and fry, stirring occasionally and scraping up the bits stuck to the pan, until golden brown and crisp – about 5 minutes.

Add the leek, carrots, celery, cabbage and crushed garlic. Give it all a good stir, then cook for 5 minutes.

Add the tomatoes, tomato purée, cannellini beans, stock and Parmesan rind and stir again. Bring the soup to the boil, then cover and simmer gently for 30 minutes.

Meanwhile, preheat the oven to 200°C, 180°C fan (400°F), Gas Mark 6.

Drizzle the ciabatta halves with the extra olive oil and place them on a baking sheet. Toast in the oven until golden brown – about 5 minutes.

Rub one side of the toasts with the remaining garlic clove, then place each toast in an individual soup bowl.

Ladle the soup over the toasts, sprinkle with the Parmesan and parsley and serve straight away. *Semplice e buono*!

ZUPPA DI POLLO

SERVES 4

2 tablespoons olive oil
7 carrots, roughly chopped
7 celery sticks, roughly
   chopped
1 large onion, unpeeled
   and unchopped
1 large chicken (about
   1.7kg/3lb 12oz)
Stelline (little stars) pasta
Salt and freshly ground
   black pepper

To serve
Freshly grated
   Parmesan cheese
Handful of flat leaf
   parsley, chopped

This soup for me is simply a bowl of comfort. If you're feeling a little unwell, or it's a cold and rainy day, it always hits the spot. The whole, unpeeled onion adds a lovely golden colour, to make this soup even more warming. *Anna*

Put the oil into a very large saucepan over a medium heat, add the chopped carrots and celery and the whole onion, then fry for 5 minutes, until the carrots and celery start to soften.

Now add the chicken and just enough cold water to cover it. Bring slowly to the boil, then partially cover and simmer for 2 hours. From time to time, skim off any scum that rises to the surface, and top up the water if necessary to keep the chicken submerged.

Remove the whole onion and discard. Keeping the soup on a low heat so it stays warm, transfer the bird to a chopping board and set aside for about 15 minutes. When cool enough to handle, shred the meat, discarding the skin and bones. Set aside.

Cook the pasta in a pan of boiling salted water until al dente. Drain, then add to the soup along with the shredded chicken. Season with salt and pepper.

Ladle the soup into bowls, sprinkle with the Parmesan and parsley and serve straight away.

CRESPELLE CON SPINACI E PROSCIUTTO

MAKES 6

125g (4½oz) plain flour
2 eggs
125ml (4fl oz) milk
125ml (4fl oz) water
¼ teaspoon salt
2 tablespoons butter, melted
Sunflower oil, for frying

For the béchamel sauce
60g (2¼oz) butter
60g (2¼oz) plain flour
600ml (20fl oz) milk
1 teaspoon ground nutmeg
Salt and freshly ground black pepper

For the filling
250g (9oz) fresh spinach leaves
1 tablespoon olive oil
1 onion, finely chopped
250g (9oz) ricotta cheese
140g (5oz) mascarpone cheese
160g (5¾oz) Parma ham, roughly chopped
200g (7oz) Parmesan cheese, grated

This is a new-found favourite of mine, and it was Anna, of course, who taught me how to make it. We have a lot of fun flipping pancakes, glass of wine in hand and Italian music in the background. *Gregg*

Put the flour into a large mixing bowl, add the eggs and whisk together. Now add the milk and water, stirring to combine. Add the salt and butter, and mix again until smooth. Transfer the batter to a jug and set aside.

Put a drizzle of oil into a frying pan over a medium-high heat. When hot, tilt the pan to spread the oil around, then pour in a little batter. Gently tilt the pan again so that the batter coats the surface thinly and evenly. You will need to make 6 pancakes, so don't be over-generous.

Cook the crepe for about 2 minutes, until the underside is a nice golden brown colour. Loosen with a spatula, flip it over and cook the other side for 2 minutes. Place on a plate and keep warm. Cook the rest of the crepes in the same way, placing greaseproof paper between them to prevent them from sticking together.

To make the béchamel, melt the butter in a saucepan over a medium-low heat, then stir in the flour. Whisk in the milk a bit at a time, stirring continuously until the mixture thickens and you have a smooth sauce. Stir in the nutmeg, then remove from the heat and season with salt and pepper. Cover the surface directly with clingfilm to prevent a skin forming, and set aside.

To make the filling, place the spinach and a splash of water in a saucepan over a medium heat and cook for a few minutes, stirring from time to time. When the spinach has wilted, drain very well, then squeeze dry in kitchen paper or a clean cloth to remove any remaining water. (You don't want soggy pancakes.) Set aside.

Put the olive oil into a clean saucepan over a medium heat. When hot, add the onion and fry for a few minutes, until soft.

Place the ricotta and mascarpone in a large bowl and add the cooked onion, the Parma ham, 150g (5½oz) of the Parmesan and some salt and pepper. Mix well.

Preheat the oven to 200°C, 180°C fan (400°F), Gas Mark 6. Butter an ovenproof baking dish about 26 x 20 cm (10½ x 8 inches).

Place one crepe in front of you and spread 2 heaped tablespoons of the filling in the middle. Roll it up and place in the prepared dish, seam-side down. Repeat this step until you have filled and rolled all your crepes.

Pour the béchamel sauce all over the crepes, then sprinkle with the remaining Parmesan. Bake for 25–30 minutes, or until golden brown on top. *Delizioso*!

MELANZANE PARMIGIANA

SERVES 4

Olive oil, for frying
   and rubbing
1 onion, finely chopped
1 garlic clove, grated
   or chopped
700g (1lb 9oz) passata
1 teaspoon dried oregano
2 large aubergines, thinly
   sliced lengthways
100g (3½oz) Parmesan
   cheese, grated
70g (2½oz) mozzarella
   cheese, grated
Salt

I first had this dish over 20 years ago on one of my first trips to Italy. It's a staple of the south, where people love their veg as much as I do. *Gregg*

Preheat the oven to 190°C, 170°C fan (375°F), Gas Mark 5.

Place a glug of olive oil into a saucepan over a medium heat, add the onion and garlic and fry for a few minutes, until softened. Add the passata and oregano, season with salt and cook for 5–10 minutes, until the sauce has thickened. Set aside.

Place a frying pan or griddle pan over a medium-high heat. Rub the aubergine slices on both sides with olive oil, then place in the hot pan to soften. This will take roughly 2 minutes per side.

Take an ovenproof baking dish about 26 x 20cm (10½ x 8 inches) and pour in just enough of the tomato sauce to cover the base. Sprinkle with about a quarter of the Parmesan, then cover with some of your aubergine slices. Make more layers of sauce, Parmesan and aubergine, until you have used them all up. Sprinkle the top with the mozzarella, cover with foil and place in the oven for 30 minutes.

Remove the foil, turn the oven to its highest setting and bake the dish for another 5 minutes, until the top is bubbling and golden.

COURGETTE OMELETTE

FRITTATA DI ZUCCHINE

SERVES 2-4

Olive oil, for frying
1 onion, chopped
350g (12oz) courgettes,
    chopped
6 eggs
50g (1¾oz) Parmesan
    cheese, grated (add
    more or less to taste)
Salt and freshly ground
    black pepper

So light, so easy, so cheap. How healthy you want this dish
to be depends on how much Parmesan you put in. *Gregg*

Place a frying pan over a medium heat, add a glug of olive
oil and fry the onion and courgettes until brown. Set aside.

Beat the eggs in a bowl, and season with salt and pepper.
Add the Parmesan, cooked courgettes and onion and mix well.

Pour the egg mixture into the frying pan and cook over a
medium heat for 5 minutes.

Meanwhile, preheat the grill. Place the pan under the grill for
another 5 minutes, until the top becomes puffy and golden.
Serve straight away.

PASTA FATTA IN CASA

SERVES 4-6

600g (1lb 5oz) "00" flour,
    plus extra for dusting
3 large eggs plus 3 large
    egg yolks
2 tablespoons olive oil
Salt

Pasta is such a large part of our family that we all have a particular memory of it. Dad's mum taught him how to make it. Mum's mum taught her how to make it. My nonna taught me how to make it, and then I taught my husband. It's amazing stuff and brings the whole family together. *Anna*

Tip the flour onto a clean work surface and season with a pinch of salt. Using your fist, make a deep well in the centre of it.

Break the eggs into a jug, add the extra yolks and 1 tablespoon olive oil and whisk together until combined. Gradually pour this mixture into the well while using the fingers of one hand in a circular motion to work the flour into the liquid. (If you don't want to get messy, you can do the mixing with a fork.) At first, the mixture will be soft and crumbly, but it will gradually come together as a ball of dough. If it feels too dry, add a few drops of water; if it feels too wet, add a little more flour. It is difficult to be precise because the humidity of the room will affect the moisture in the flour. Just take care when adding water because if you add too much and then have to add more flour, it can make the pasta tough.

Now, knead the dough, pressing, pulling and stretching it for a good few minutes, until it feels smooth and springs back when you press your thumb into it. This is hard work and will make your arms ache, but keep going – it's worth it.

Lightly massage the kneaded dough with the remaining olive oil, wrap it in clingfilm or a sealable plastic bag, and place it in the fridge for 30 minutes. (You may want to have a rest too.)

Remove the dough from the fridge – it should feel softer and more elastic –and cut it into 4 equal pieces.

Set your pasta machine to the thickest setting (usually "0") and lightly flour the roller. Take one piece of dough, flatten it into a circle and feed it through the roller. Repeat this step twice more. Fold the dough as if you are folding a letter, and press it between your hands. This will make a rectangular shape. Feed the pasta through the machine once or twice more, until it's smooth and becoming longer.

Now change the machine setting to "1" and pass the dough through it twice. Continue working your way up the settings, passing the dough through twice on each one. Don't be tempted to skip any settings or the pasta will tear and snag. If your pasta becomes too long to manage, lay it on a chopping board and cut it in half.

Roll the pasta as thinly as needed for the shape you are making. For example, if making tagliatelle, I would go up to setting "5" on the machine.

Cut the pasta into your desired shape. Place on a floured baking tray and sprinkle flour on top to keep it dry while you bring a large pan of salted water to the boil. Add the pasta and cook for 4 minutes, or until al dente. Drain and enjoy with your preferred sauce.

SALSA DI POMODORO

SERVES 4

3 tablespoons extra
  virgin olive oil
2 garlic cloves, kept whole
1 tablespoon tomato purée
800g (1lb 12oz) passata
Large bunch of fresh basil,
  stems tied together
2 teaspoons salt
2 teaspoons sugar

My nonna would get a bottle of homemade passata and make this very simple pasta sauce while we chatted. I would have the job of tearing open a packet of pasta and cooking it. We would then sit outside and share this simple meal. Simplicity, of course, is the beauty of *cucina Italia*. *Rina*

Put the olive oil into a saucepan over a medium-high heat and fry the garlic cloves for 1–2 minutes, until pale golden all over. Discard the garlic – you just need the flavoured oil.

Lower the heat, add the tomato purée to the pan and fry for a minute or so, stirring to make sure it doesn't catch and burn.

Pour in the passata and give it a good stir. Add the bunch of basil, the salt and sugar, and simmer for 20 minutes, stirring occasionally. The sauce will start to bubble like a volcano.

Remove the basil and serve the sauce with your preferred pasta shape.

LASAGNE

SERVES 4–6

Olive oil, for frying
750g (1lb 9oz) minced
    beef
500g (1lb 2oz) minced
    pork
4 carrots, cut into chunks
4 celery sticks, cut into
    chunks
4 onions, cut into chunks
2 garlic cloves
4 tablespoons tomato
    purée
2 x 500g (1lb 2oz) cartons
    passata
12 lasagne sheets
100g (3½oz) Parmesan
    cheese, grated
250g (9oz) mozzarella
    cheese, grated
Salt

My mamma put a lot of love into this dish when I was a child. It wasn't something she made regularly, only when she had time. Because it was special to her it became special to me. *Rina*

Put a glug of oil into a frying pan placed over a medium-high heat. When hot, brown the minced beef and pork in batches. Drain the mince in a sieve to remove any excess oil. Set aside.

Put the carrots, celery, onions and garlic into a food processor and blitz them into small pieces. You can chop them by hand if you wish, but using a processor gets the vegetables really fine so that they dissolve and thicken the sauce nicely.

Put a glug of oil into a large saucepan over a medium heat. When hot, add the chopped vegetables and fry for about 15 minutes, until softened.

Stir in the tomato purée and cook for a few minutes. Add the browned meat to the pan, pour in the passata, season with salt and cook on a low heat, partially covered, for 2 hours. Set the ragù aside to cool for 30 minutes.

Preheat the oven to 180°C, 160°C fan (350°F), Gas Mark 4.

Take a 23 x 30cm (9 x 12 inch) ovenproof dish and ladle a thin layer of the ragù inside it. Cover with a layer of lasagne sheets, overlapping them slightly and snapping them to fit. Add another layer of ragù and sprinkle with Parmesan. Repeat this layering process twice more, finishing with a layer of ragù.

Cover the dish with foil and bake for 35 minutes. Discard the foil, sprinkle the lasagne with the mozzarella and return to the oven for 15 minutes, until the cheese is bubbling and golden.

Leave the lasagne to rest for 30 minutes before serving – it's worth it because you will have a nice slice of it rather than a plate of slop.

SPAGHETTI ALLE VONGOLE

SERVES 4–6

1kg (2lb 4oz) clams
3 tablespoons plain flour
500g (1lb 2oz) spaghetti
3 tablespoons butter
2 tablespoons olive oil,
    plus extra for drizzling
2 garlic cloves, kept whole
½ onion, finely chopped
½ glass (75ml/2½fl oz)
    dry white wine
30g (1oz) flat leaf
    parsley, chopped
Juice of ½ lemon
Salt

When I was working as a lifeguard, Rina and I would regularly go to a small seaside restaurant where the spaghetti alle vongole was so delicious we still talk about it to this day. I love to cook this dish – it's the taste of the sea in a bowl. *Massimo*

Place the clams in a large glass bowl, cover with cold water and stir in a handful of salt. Add 1 tablespoon flour (this acts as a cleaning agent and removes any grit) and stir. Set aside for 1 hour.

Using a slotted spoon, transfer the clams to a plate and discard the water in the bowl along with any sand at the bottom. Rinse the bowl and repeat the soaking process until the clams no longer release any sand (this should take no more than 3 times). Discard any clams that are wide open and refuse to close when tapped. Drain and set aside.

Bring a large pan of lightly salted water to the boil (the clams are already salty, so you won't need as much salt as usual). Add the spaghetti and cook for 10–12 minutes, until al dente. Drain, reserving half a cup of the cooking water. Set aside.

Meanwhile, heat the butter and olive oil in a pan large enough to eventually hold all the clams and spaghetti. Add the garlic cloves and fry, stirring often, until pale and golden. Discard them once they have flavoured the butter and oil.

Add the onion and fry for a few minutes, until softened. Pour in the wine, add the clams and increase the heat to high. Cover the pan with a lid and cook until the clams open and release their juices, 3–6 minutes, depending on the size of the clams.

Pour a quarter of the reserved pasta water into the pan and bring to the boil. Add the cooked spaghetti and stir. Cook over a high heat for 2 minutes, stirring constantly, until some of the juices have been soaked up. Sprinkle in the parsley, drizzle with olive oil and stir again. Add more pasta water if the sauce seems dry, and cook for another minute or two. Serve in deep bowls along with the lemon juice, for drizzling. *Buon appetito*!

SPAGHETTI ALLA CARBONARA

SERVES 4

500g (1lb 2oz) spaghetti
3 tablespoons olive oil
50g (1¾oz) smoked
    pancetta cubes
3 eggs
100g (3½oz) Parmesan
    cheese, grated
Freshly ground black
    pepper

Some countries have taken to adding cream to this dish, but that is never done in Italy. *Anna*

Cook the spaghetti in a large pan of boiling salted water until al dente, 10–12 minutes.

Meanwhile, heat the oil in a frying pan and fry the pancetta cubes until they are crisp and browned.

Beat the eggs in a large bowl. Add the Parmesan, season with pepper and mix again.

Drain the pasta and add it to the pan containing the pancetta. Give it a good stir to coat in the oil, then set aside to cool for 5 minutes. This is necessary so that the egg doesn't scramble when it is added.

Once the pasta has cooled slightly, stir in the egg and cheese mixture until the spaghetti is well coated. Serve straight away.

SPAGHETTI AGLIO OLIO PEPERONCINO

SERVES 4

500g (1lb 2oz) spaghetti
100ml (3½fl oz) olive oil,
　plus extra for drizzling
　if necessary
4 garlic cloves, grated
1 teaspoon dried
　chilli flakes
Salt
2 tablespoons chopped
　flat leaf parsley,
　to serve

This recipe is super quick and super tasty, hardly any effort to make. It was one of my dad's favourite pasta dishes. *Massimo*

Cook the spaghetti in a large pan of boiling salted water until al dente, 10–12 minutes.

Meanwhile, place a frying pan over a medium–high heat, add the olive oil, garlic, chilli flakes and a pinch of salt and cook for 2–3 minutes, stirring with a wooden spoon.

Drain the pasta, reserving half a cup of the cooking water. Add both pasta and water to the frying pan and stir to make a nice sauce. Use two forks to toss the spaghetti so that it's fully coated in the garlic chilli oil. If it seems a bit dry, you can add some extra olive oil.

Sprinkle the chopped parsley over the pasta and serve.

LINGUINE DI GRANCHIO

SERVES 4

2 tablespoons olive oil
2 shallots, diced
1 garlic clove, grated
500g (1lb 2oz) linguine
Juice of 1 lemon
30g (1oz) butter
600g (1lb 5oz) fresh,
    cooked crab meat
4 tablespoons chopped
    flat leaf parsley

Cooking this recipe is so enjoyable. The crab smells like the sea and the lemon squeezed over at the end gives it a wonderful lift. The whole dish brings to mind a summer lunch by the sea with a glass of white wine. *Anna*

Heat the olive oil in a frying pan and fry the shallots for a few minutes, until softened. Add the garlic and cook for another minute.

Cook the linguine in a large saucepan of boiling salted water for about 12 minutes, until al dente. Drain, reserving half a cup of the cooking water. Add the pasta and water to the frying pan.

Add the lemon juice and butter, increase the heat a little and cook for 2 minutes.

Flake in the crab meat, stir gently and warm through for about 4 minutes. Any longer and it will be spoiled. Sprinkle with the chopped parsley, then transfer to serving bowls and enjoy!

RAVIOLI CON GRANCHIO E GAMBERO

SERVES 4

4 eggs
400g (14oz) "00" flour
1 tablespoon olive oil
1 teaspoon salt
4 tablespoons water,
    if required

For the filling
50g (1¾oz) cooked
    brown crab meat
50g (1¾oz) cooked
    white crab meat
50g (1¾oz) cooked
    prawns, finely chopped
1 egg
1 tablespoon finely
    chopped flat leaf parsley
1 teaspoon lemon zest
Salt and freshly ground
    black pepper

To serve
Knob of butter
Freshly grated
    Parmesan cheese

These crab ravioli are delicate and deliciously flavoured little parcels, perfect for a dinner party. They take a little patience to put together, but the result is well worth the effort. *Anna*

_____

Break the eggs into a bowl and beat with a fork until smooth.

Put the flour onto a chopping board or work surface, or into a bowl if you prefer. Make a well in the centre, pour in the beaten eggs and use the tips of your fingers or a fork to mix them together and form a ball of dough. If it feels too dry, add a few drops of water; if it feels too wet, add a little more flour. Be careful when adding water: if you add too much, your dough will be wet and you will have to add more flour, which can make the pasta tough.

Now you have to knead the dough, pressing, pulling and stretching it for a good few minutes, until it feels smooth rather than grainy and floury. This is hard work, but worth it. Cover it with clingfilm and place in the fridge for at least 30 minutes.

Once the dough has chilled, combine all the filling ingredients in a large bowl and mix well.

Cut the chilled dough into 4 equal pieces. Take one piece at a time, keeping the rest covered, and flatten with a rolling pin into a 13cm (5 inch) square. Set your pasta machine to the thickest setting (usually "0") and lightly flour the roller. Feed the square of dough through the roller. Repeat this step twice more. Fold the dough as if folding a letter, and press it between your hands to make a rectangular shape. Feed the pasta through the machine once or twice more, until it's smooth and becoming longer.

Now change the machine setting to "1" and pass the dough through it twice. Continue working your way up the settings, passing the dough through twice on each one. Don't be tempted to skip any settings or the pasta will tear and snag. For ravioli you will need to go up to number "6". If your pasta becomes too long to manage, lay it on a chopping board and cut it in half.

Set out a floured ravioli form, a mould consisting of two pieces – one with holes and the other with domes that fit inside them. Place a sheet of pasta over the holed part, then gently press down with the domed part to push the pasta into the holes. Place a teaspoonful of the filling in each pasta indentation.

Place a second sheet of dough over the filling, then use a rolling pin to roll over the form. This will press on the serrated edges around the ravioli and cut them out. Peel off the excess pasta and tip the ravioli out of the form. Repeat with the remaining dough and filling.

Cook the ravioli in a large pan of boiling salted water for about 4 minutes. Drain and serve with a knob of butter and a sprinkling of Parmesan.

RAVIOLI CON PISELLI E PANCETTA

SERVES 4

1 quantity ravioli pasta
  (see pages 98–9)

For the filling
Olive oil, for frying
50g (1¾oz) pancetta
  cubes
100g (3½oz) peas
50g (1¾oz) ricotta cheese
Salt and freshly ground
  black pepper

To serve
Knob of butter
Freshly grated
  Parmesan cheese

Handmade ravioli always impresses people, and it's easier to make than you think. Here, the salty pancetta works really well with the sweetness from the peas. *Gregg*

To make the filling, put a glug of olive oil into a frying pan and fry the pancetta until browned. Set aside.

Cook the peas in boiling salted water for 3 minutes, then drain. Tumble them into a blender and blitz to a coarse purée. Pour into a bowl and leave to cool slightly.

Once the purée has cooled, add the ricotta, pancetta, and some salt and pepper, then give it a good stir. Your filling is now ready.

Make the ravioli with a mould (see pages 98–9), then cook them in a large pan of boiling salted water for about 4 minutes. Drain and serve with a knob of butter and a sprinkling of Parmesan.

CANNELLONI DI SPINACI E RICOTTA

SERVES 4

12 cannelloni tubes
150g (5½oz) mozzarella
    cheese, grated
4 tablespoons grated
    Parmesan cheese

For the sauce
1 tablespoon olive oil
1 onion, finely chopped
1 garlic clove, crushed
700g (1lb 9oz) passata
Small handful of basil
    leaves

For the filling
300g (10½oz) spinach
500g (1lb 2oz) ricotta
    cheese
4 tablespoons grated
    Parmesan cheese
1 egg, beaten
Pinch of ground nutmeg
Salt and freshly ground
    black pepper

A beautiful dish and gloriously messy to make. Anna and I have different filling techniques: she likes to hold her cannelloni upright and fill from the top, pushing it down; I favour sticking the tube into the bowl of filling and shoving it in with my finger. *Gregg*

Start by making the sauce. Put the oil into a saucepan over a medium heat and fry the onion and garlic for a few minutes, until softened. Pour in the passata, add the basil and season with salt and pepper. Cook for 20 minutes, then set aside.

To make the filling, put the spinach into a saucepan with a splash of water and place over a medium heat for 5 minutes, stirring from time to time, until wilted. Drain in a sieve, then transfer to a tea towel and squeeze really well to remove any excess water. Place the spinach on a board and chop very finely.

Place the ricotta in a bowl, add the Parmesan, egg, nutmeg and spinach, season with salt and pepper and mix well.

Preheat the oven to 180°C, 160°C fan (350°F), Gas Mark 4.

Set out an ovenproof baking dish about 23 x 30cm (9 x 12 inches). Add a ladleful of the tomato sauce and spread it out evenly. This will prevent the pasta from sticking.

Using a spoon or your fingers, push the filling into the cannelloni tubes, then transfer them to the baking dish.

Cover the tubes with the tomato sauce. Sprinkle the mozzarella and Parmesan over the top, then cover with foil and bake for 30 minutes.

Remove the foil, turn the oven to its highest setting and bake the dish for a further 5–10 minutes, until the surface is crisp and golden brown. Allow to rest for 20 minutes before serving.

GNOCCHI ALLA ROMANA

SERVES 4

3 eggs
200g (7oz) semolina
500ml (18fl oz) whole milk
60g (2¼oz) fontina
  cheese, cubed
Olive oil, for sprinkling
60g (2¼oz) butter, cubed,
  plus extra for greasing
60g (2¼oz) Parmesan
  cheese, grated

You are probably familiar with potato gnocchi, but these ones are made with semolina and are far lighter. This recipe comes from Nonna and, from what I can make out, was possibly handed down through many generations before her. *Gregg*

Crack the eggs into a bowl, beat well, then stir in the semolina until mixed very well. Add the milk bit by bit, whisking as you go, until you have a smooth mixture. Stir in the fontina.

Place the mixture in a large saucepan over a medium heat and stir constantly with a wooden spoon for 5–7 minutes, or until very thick. Take care as the mixture may bubble and spit.

Sprinkle a baking tray with some oil and a little water. Spoon the cheese mixture into it and flatten out with a wet spatula until roughly 1cm (½ inch) thick. Allow the mixture to cool completely.

Preheat the oven to 220°C, 200°C fan (425°F), Gas Mark 7. Butter a 26 x 20cm (10½ x 8 inches) ovenproof dish.

Using a round 6cm (2½ inch) cutter, stamp out about 22 gnocchi. Arrange them in overlapping rows in the dish, a bit like roof tiles. Place a few cubes of butter in between the gnocchi and top with the rest of the butter. Sprinkle over the Parmesan and bake for 20 minutes, or until golden. Serve hot.

RISOTTO MILANESE

SERVES 2

1 litre (35fl oz)
   chicken stock
100g (3½oz) butter,
   plus an extra knob,
   to serve
1 shallot, finely diced
200g (7oz) risotto rice
Pinch of saffron strands
125ml (4fl oz) white wine
50g (1¾oz) Parmesan
   cheese, grated
Salt

On one occasion Anna and I were given some saffron by the owner of a villa where we were staying, so we made this classic risotto. It takes a while to cook, but that's OK – just open a bottle of wine and play some ABBA. The smell of saffron coming up from the pan will be amazing. *Gregg*

Pour the stock into a large saucepan and bring to a simmer over a medium heat.

Meanwhile, melt the butter in a heavy-based saucepan and fry the shallot for a few minutes, until softened but not brown. Add the rice and stir until well coated, then cook for 6 minutes, stirring all the time with a wooden spoon. Sprinkle in the saffron and watch the rice take on a beautiful golden colour. Pour in the wine and let it bubble for about 2 minutes.

Start adding the hot chicken stock a ladleful at a time, stirring until it's absorbed. Keep doing this until all the liquid has been absorbed and the rice is creamy but still has a slight crunch; this should take no longer than 25 minutes.

Before serving, stir in a large knob of butter and the grated Parmesan and season with salt.

RISOTTO AL NERO DI SEPPIA

SERVES 4

1.2 litres (40fl oz)
    fish stock
35g (1¼oz) butter
2 tablespoons olive oil
2 shallots, finely chopped
300ml (10fl oz) white wine
2 x 4g sachets squid ink
300g (10½oz) risotto rice
250g (9oz) squid rings
    (ask your fishmonger
    for squid tubes and then
    cut into rings about 1cm
    (½ inch) wide)
Handful of flat leaf
    parsley, chopped

The colours of this dish are striking: jet black grains of rice with vibrant green parsley. If you want to impress your guests, this one is a must. *Anna*

Put the fish stock into a pan and bring it to a gentle simmer.

Meanwhile, melt the butter in a heavy-based saucepan along with the olive oil and fry the shallots for a few minutes, until softened. Pour in the wine and allow it to bubble until slightly reduced. Add the squid ink and watch the liquid turn jet black. Add the rice and stir until well coated.

Start adding the hot fish stock a ladleful at a time, stirring until it's absorbed. Keep doing this until all the liquid has been absorbed and the rice is creamy but still has a slight crunch; this should take no longer than 30 minutes.

Toward the end of the cooking time, add the squid rings, stir well and cook for 1–2 minutes until firm – any longer and you will end up with very chewy rubber.

Sprinkle the risotto with chopped parsley and serve straight away.

RISOTTO AI FUNGHI

SERVES 2–3

60g (2¼oz) dried porcini
    mushrooms
2 litres (70fl oz) hot water
Olive oil, for frying
80g (2¾oz) butter
1 onion, finely chopped
400g (14oz) risotto rice
150ml (5fl oz) white wine
50g (1¾oz) Parmesan
    cheese, grated
Salt and freshly ground
    black pepper

Traditionally, risotto is a dish from northern Italy because it's one of the few areas that can successfully grow rice. It's not particularly popular in the south, but you do come across it. Personally, I don't care where I am when I eat it. *Gregg*

Place the porcini in a large bowl, add the water and cover with clingfilm. Leave to soak overnight, or for at least 5 hours.

Drain the porcini, reserving the water (it's worth then pouring the reserved liquid through a sieve lined with a sheet of kitchen paper to get rid of any grit from the mushrooms). Squeeze the mushrooms dry, then roughly chop. Put a glug of olive oil into a frying pan and cook the mushrooms for 10–12 minutes. Season with salt and pepper, then set aside.

Place the reserved porcini water in a pan and bring to a gentle simmer.

Meanwhile, melt the butter in a saucepan over a low-medium heat. Add the onion and cook for a few minutes without colouring until soft. Tumble in the rice, stir to coat with the butter, and cook for about 8 minutes. Add the wine and let it bubble for a few minutes.

Start adding the hot porcini water a ladleful at a time, stirring until it's absorbed. Keep doing this until all the water has been absorbed and the rice is creamy but still has a slight crunch; this should take no longer than 30 minutes.

Add the cooked porcini to the risotto, sprinkle with the Parmesan and give it a good stir before serving.

GAMBERI CON PEPERONCINO E AGLIO

SERVES 4-6

3 tablespoons olive oil
3 garlic cloves, chopped
1 teaspoon chilli flakes
28 raw large king prawns
  with shells on
300ml (10fl oz) dry
  white wine
3 tablespoons finely
  chopped flat leaf
  parsley

I can remember watching my dad make this recipe, and being fascinated by the grey prawns turning pink as they cooked. They tasted so good that I even sucked the juices from the heads. It's a messy dish to eat – you will have napkins covered in pink once you have finished – but so worth it. *Anna*

Put the oil in a frying pan, add the garlic and chilli flakes and fry over a medium heat for 2–3 minutes.

Add the prawns and cook, stirring, for 2–3 minutes until they turn pink.

Increase the heat, pour in the wine and allow to bubble for 1 minute so that the alcohol evaporates.

Sprinkle the prawns with the chopped parsley, then tumble them into a large serving dish.

Serve with crusty bread to mop up all the lovely juices.

FRITTO MISTO DI MARE

SERVES 2–3

1 litre (35fl oz)
  sunflower oil
1 x 350g (12oz) bag
  mixed frozen seafood
  (we use whitebait,
  prawns, squid and
  sardine fillets)
150g (5½oz) plain flour
1 egg
200ml (7fl oz)
  sparkling water
Salt and freshly ground
  black pepper
1 lemon, to serve

My sister Flora lives near the coast in Italy, where there is an abundance of shellfish. I always think of her making mountains of fried seafood for the whole family to enjoy, along with lots of wine and chat. *Massimo*

Pour the oil into a deep saucepan and place over a medium-high heat.

Meanwhile, place the seafood in a colander and rinse under running water to defrost it. Leave to dry on a clean tea towel – if this isn't done, the excess moisture will lead to a soggy batter.

Place the flour in a bowl, add some salt and pepper, then crack in the egg. Whisk until thoroughly combined. Add the sparkling water and whisk again; the batter with fizz and bubble slightly.

Tumble the seafood into the batter and mix well. Line a large plate with kitchen paper.

When the oil reaches 180°C (350°F), or a piece of batter sizzles on contact with it, start frying the seafood in small batches. Lift the pieces with your fingers, allowing the excess batter to drip off, then slowly lower them into the hot oil, being careful not to crowd the pan and make it bubble over. Using a slotted spoon, gently move the seafood around to ensure it doesn't clump together, and fry for 2–3 minutes, or until crisp and golden brown. Transfer to the prepared plate and keep warm. Cook the rest of the seafood in the same way.

Serve with a sprinkle of salt and a squeeze of lemon. *Delizioso*!

VITELLO TONNATO

SERVES 2

Olive oil, for frying
6 slices of thinly cut veal,
  about 140g (5oz) each
200g (7oz) canned
  tuna, drained
3 canned anchovies,
  drained
2 teaspoons capers
Juice of ½ lemon
6 tablespoons
  mayonnaise
Salt
Handful of rocket,
  to serve

Tuna and veal might sound like an odd combination, but it tastes wonderful and is actually one of my favourite dishes. I think it's all about the flavour of the sauce – the veal is just there to provide texture. *Gregg*

Put a glug of oil into a large frying pan over a high heat and fry the veal for 1–2 minutes on each side. The thinner the slices, the less cooking they need.

Place the tuna, anchovies, capers, lemon juice and mayonnaise in a blender and blitz until you have a creamy but slightly rough sauce. Add salt to taste – remember that the anchovies and capers are already salty, so taste before you add more.

Place the veal on plates and spoon the tuna sauce over the top. Add some rocket and enjoy with some crusty bread to scoop up the tasty sauce.

Chapter Three

SECOND
COURSES

ZUPPA DI PESCE

SERVES 4

2 tablespoons olive oil
2 garlic cloves, finely
    chopped
½ tsp chilli flakes
    (optional)
160g (5¾oz) tomato purée
500g (1lb 2oz) assorted
    fish and seafood (cod,
    haddock, squid, prawns,
    mussels, clams, etc.),
    chopped into chunks
100ml (3½fl oz)
    white wine
300ml (10fl oz) fish stock
1 teaspoon dried oregano
Salt
Large handful of flat
    leaf parsley, chopped,
    to serve

Here we have classic Italian flavours married to marvellous fish and seafood. I love dunking chunks of warm crusty bread into this soup: the perfect hearty second course. *Massimo*

Put the olive oil into a large saucepan and fry the garlic, chilli flakes (if using) and tomato purée over a medium heat for a couple of minutes.

Add your fish and seafood and cook, stirring, for about 1 minute. Pour in the wine and cook for another 3–5 minutes, until the wine has reduced slightly.

Add the stock and oregano, stir well and add salt to taste. Bring to the boil, then simmer for 25–30 minutes.

Sprinkle over the chopped parsley and serve with warm crusty bread.

PASTA CON FAGIOLI

SERVES 4

Olive oil, for frying
   and drizzling
2 onions, finely chopped
2 carrots, finely chopped
2 celery sticks, finely
   chopped
2 garlic cloves, grated
130g (4½oz) smoked
   pancetta cubes
150ml (5fl oz) white wine
2 x 400g (14oz) cans
   cannellini beans,
   rinsed and drained
2 x 400g (14oz) cans
   borlotti beans, rinsed
   and drained
1.2 litres (40fl oz)
   chicken stock
300g (10½oz) dried
   ditalini rigati pasta
   or macaroni
Salt and freshly ground
   black pepper
Handful of flat leaf
   parsley, chopped,
   to serve

Although a pasta dish, this recipe is filling and satisfying enough to make a great second course. It is also a good way of using up any oddments of pasta and cans of beans that are lurking at the back of your cupboards. We always try not to waste anything. *Anna*

Preheat the oven to 200°C, 180°C fan (400°F), Gas Mark 6.

Put a glug of olive oil into a frying pan over a medium heat and fry the onions, carrots, celery, garlic and pancetta for about 5 minutes, until the vegetables have softened. Pour in the wine and let it bubble for about 5 minutes, until the alcohol has evaporated. Tumble in the beans, add the stock and stir together. Transfer to an ovenproof, lidded casserole dish and place in the oven for 1½ hours.

Cook the pasta in boiling salted water for about 10 minutes, or until al dente. Drain well, then add to the beans and stir. Season with salt and pepper, sprinkle the parsley over the surface and add a drizzle of olive oil before serving.

PIZZA DI PATATE CON PROSCIUTTO E FORMAGGIO

SERVES 4

Olive oil, for greasing
150g (5½oz) dry
   breadcrumbs
1.2kg (2lb 10oz) floury
   potatoes, such
   as Desiree
2 egg yolks
70g (2½oz) Parmesan
   cheese, grated
50g (1¾oz) pecorino
   cheese, grated
150g (5½oz) cooked
   ham, chopped
250g (9oz) mozzarella
   cheese, grated
20g (¾oz) butter,
   softened

We first had potato pizzas in Naples, though they originate in Apulia. They are not pizzas in the way we might expect, with a dough base and toppings – they are actually more like cakes. In some areas they are known as "torta di patate". *Anna*

Preheat the oven to 200°C, 180°C fan (400°F), Gas Mark 6. Oil a 25cm (10 inch) cake tin, then dust with 50g (1¾oz) of the breadcrumbs.

Cook the potatoes in a large pan of boiling salted water until tender. Drain, then return them to the pan and mash well. Add the egg yolks, Parmesan and pecorino and beat in with a wooden spoon. Stir in the ham.

Spoon the potato mixture into the prepared tin and level the surface. Sprinkle with the mozzarella and remaining breadcrumbs, spread over the melted butter and bake for 40 minutes.

BASIC PIZZA DOUGH

MAKES 3 LARGE PIZZAS

14g (3 teaspoons)
 dried yeast
100ml (3½fl oz)
 warm water
1 teaspoon sugar
1 tablespoon olive oil,
 plus extra for drizzling
500g (1lb 2oz) strong
 white bread flour,
 plus extra for dusting
1 teaspoon salt
250ml (9fl oz)
 warm water

Perhaps Italy's most famous export, pizza is a simple dish that is all too easy to mess up if the basic elements aren't right. Good dough is fundamental to good pizza, and my recipe below won't let you down. Once you have the dough sorted, you can then get creative with the toppings and have great fun coming up with new combinations. However, we also include three traditional pizzas in this section because you can't beat the old favourites. Rina says I make the best pizza outside Napoli. I'm not sure I believe her, but she is kind to me. *Gregg*

Put the yeast into a small bowl with 100ml (3½fl oz) warm water, sugar and oil and give it a good mix. Cover with clingfilm and leave in a warm place for 45–60 minutes, until frothy.

Sift the flour and salt into a large bowl. Make a well in the centre and pour in the yeast mixture and 250ml (9fl oz) warm water. Use your fingers to bring it all together into a sticky dough. It will get messy, but that's part of the fun.

Turn the dough onto a floured surface and knead well for 15 minutes, pulling, stretching and rolling it until soft and silky. It's ready if it springs back when you press it with your finger.

Place a drizzle of olive oil in a large bowl, add your dough and roll it in the oil until coated. Cover with clingfilm and a tea towel and leave in a warm place for 4 hours, or until doubled in size.

Place the dough on a floured surface, divide into 3 equal pieces and roll each piece into a ball. Use the dough as required.

PIZZA MARGARITA

SERVES 1

Olive oil, for greasing
   and drizzling
Flour, for dusting
1 ball of pizza dough
   (see page 131)
225g (8oz) mozzarella
   cheese, torn or sliced
Small handful of basil
   leaves

For the basic pizza sauce
1 tablespoon olive oil
1 garlic clove
140g (5oz) passata
Salt and freshly ground
   black pepper

This classic pizza was named after the first queen of a united Italy, when she visited Naples. *Anna*

Preheat the oven to its highest setting. Oil a perforated pizza tray (the perforations will help to create a crisp base).

Next, make the sauce. Put the oil into a small pan over a medium heat and fry the garlic for a couple of minutes. Discard the garlic once it has flavoured the oil. Pour in the passata and cook for 4 minutes. Season with salt and pepper and set aside.

Lightly flour a work surface. Using a rolling pin, roll the dough into a 30cm (12 inch) circle, then place it on the prepared tray.

Spoon 3–4 tablespoons of sauce over the pizza base, leaving a clear 2cm (¾ inch) border around the edge (any remaining sauce will keep in the refrigerator for a couple of days). Dot the mozzarella and basil leaves over the surface, then drizzle with olive oil. Bake for 7–10 minutes, until the cheese is melted and bubbling.

PIZZA CAPRICCIOSA

SERVES 1

Olive oil, for greasing
and drizzling
Flour, for dusting
1 ball of pizza dough
(see page 131)
3–4 tablespoons
basic pizza sauce
(see page 133)
60g (2¼oz) mozzarella
cheese, grated
60g (2¼oz) prosciutto
or good-quality
cooked ham
60g (2¼oz) cooked
mushrooms
70g (2½oz) artichokes
in oil, drained and
cut into wedges
1 teaspoon dried oregano

I can't resist this one, honestly – ham, artichokes and oregano
are irresistible to me. *Gregg*

_____

Preheat the oven to its highest setting. Oil a perforated pizza
tray (the perforations will help to create a crisp base).

Lightly flour a work surface. Using a rolling pin, roll the dough
into a 30cm (12 inch) circle, then place it on the prepared tray.

Spoon the sauce over the pizza base, leaving a clear 2cm
(¾ inch) border around the edge.

Dot the mozzarella, prosciutto, mushrooms and artichokes
over the surface. Drizzle with olive oil and sprinkle with
the oregano. Bake for 7–10 minutes until golden brown.

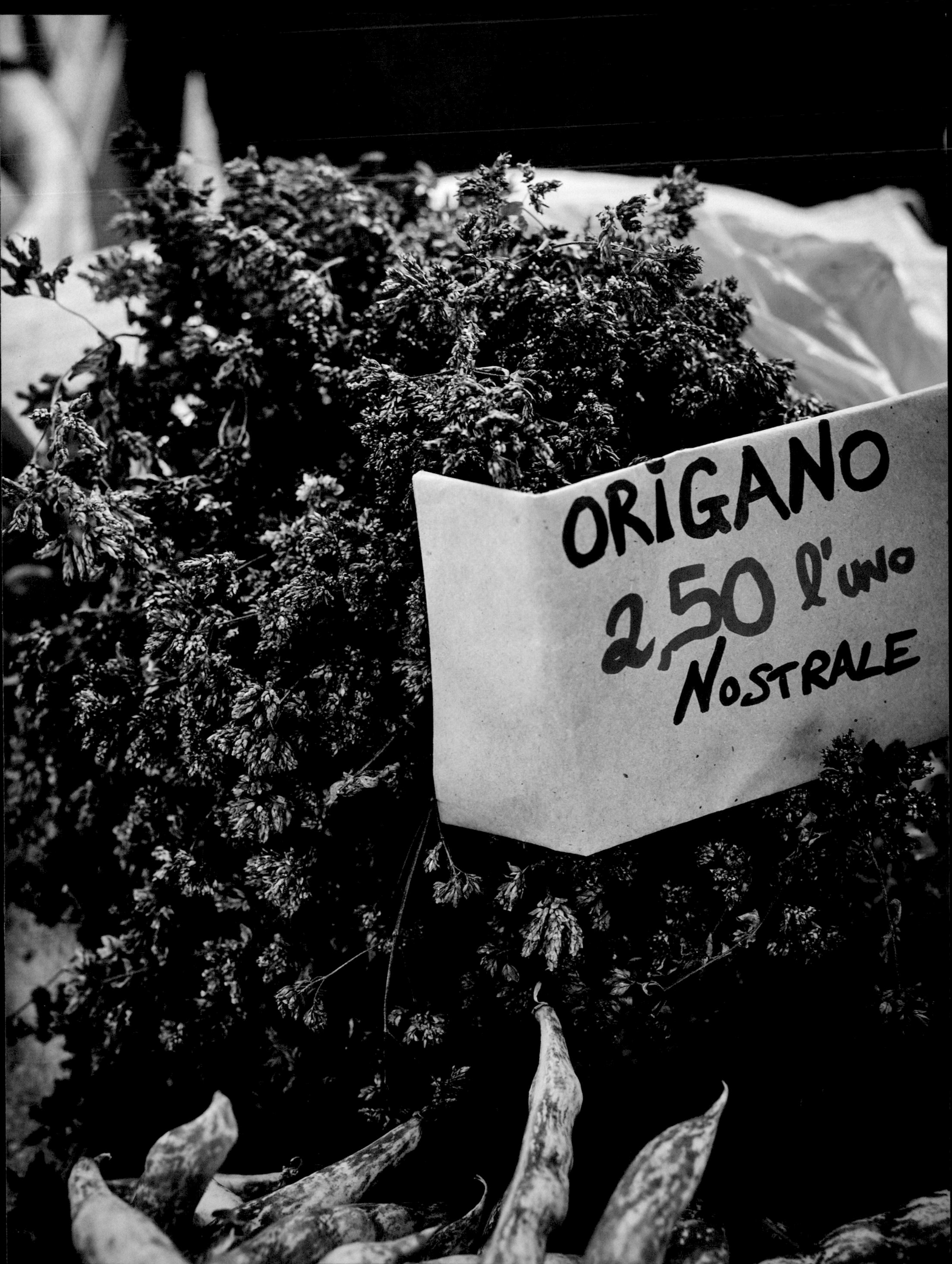
ORIGANO
2,50 l'uno
NOSTRALE

PIZZA BIANCA

SERVES 1

Olive oil, for greasing and
  drizzling
Flour, for dusting
1 ball of pizza dough
  (see page 131)
50g (1¾oz) ricotta
  cheese, drained
50g (1¾oz) provolone
  cheese, grated
50g (1¾oz) Parmesan
  cheese, grated
50g (1¾oz) pecorino
  cheese, grated
1 teaspoon dried oregano
Salt and freshly ground
  black pepper

A lovely mixture of cheeses comes together here in a gloriously creamy and mildly salty pizza. *Gregg*

Preheat the oven to its highest setting. Oil a perforated pizza tray (the perforations will help to create a crisp base).

Lightly flour a work surface. Using a rolling pin, roll the dough into a 30cm (12 inch) circle, then place it on the prepared tray.

Spoon the ricotta all over the pizza base, then spread it out, leaving a clear 2cm (¾ inch) border around the edge. Sprinkle the grated cheeses on top, followed by the oregano. Drizzle with olive oil and season with salt and pepper. Bake for 10 minutes, until the cheese has melted and turned golden brown.

CALAMARI RIPIENI

SERVES 4

4 medium-sized squid, including tentacles (ask your fishmonger to clean it)
1 garlic clove, crushed
150g (5½oz) breadcrumbs
5 tablespoons olive oil
30g (1oz) sundried tomatoes, finely chopped
Large handful of flat leaf parsley, chopped
Salt and freshly ground black pepper

It's true, squid isn't very pretty, but it's light and delicious to eat. The fishmonger will clean it for you if you like, but it's an interesting thing to do yourself. You're OK with ink and slime, aren't you? *Gregg*

Preheat the oven to 180°C, 160°C fan (350°F), Gas Mark 4.

Finely chop the squid tentacles and place them in a bowl with the garlic, breadcrumbs, olive oil, tomatoes, parsley and salt and pepper. Mix well.

Stuff the tentacle mixture into the squid tubes, securing the ends with cocktail sticks. Place them on a baking tray, cover with foil and bake for 20–25 minutes, until the flesh is opaque. Remove the foil, then return the squid to the oven for another 5 minutes, until lightly browned and crisp.

SALT COD IN TOMATO SAUCE

BACCALÀ IN SALSA DI POMODORO

SERVES 4

900g (2lb) salt cod
Olive oil, for frying
1 large onion, finely diced
700g (1lb 9oz) passata
2 tablespoons capers
Small handful of flat leaf
  parsley, chopped

In many Italian families, salt cod is served during the winter holiday season. When I first made this dish with my husband Gregg, I soaked the cod for only four hours, so we ended up with a very salty meal. I learned from this that it's best to soak the salt cod overnight. *Anna*

Start this recipe a day before you want to eat it. Put the salt cod into a bowl, cover it with cold water and leave to soak for 24 hours, changing the water every 2 hours whenever possible.

Drain the cod, cut it into 5cm (2 inch) chunks and pat dry with kitchen paper. Set aside.

Preheat the oven to 200°C, 180°C fan (400°F), Gas Mark 6.

Put a glug of olive oil into a heavy-based saucepan and fry the onion for a few minutes, until softened. Pour in the passata, add the capers and cook over a medium heat for 10 minutes.

Take an ovenproof baking dish about 25 x 15cm (10 x 6 inches) and spread 3–4 tablespoons of the tomato sauce evenly across the bottom. Arrange the cod on top, then pour the remaining sauce all over it. Cover the dish with foil and bake for 20 minutes, until the cod is cooked through.

To serve, sprinkle with the parsley and eat with crusty bread.

PESCE AL FORNO

SERVES 4

8 fillets of firm
    white fish
Olive oil, for drizzling
½ head of fennel,
    thinly sliced
8 small sprigs of flat
    leaf parsley
20 pitted black olives
20 cherry tomatoes,
    sliced in half
Salt and freshly ground
    black pepper

No matter what kind of fish you buy, this is a fantastic and easy way of cooking it. *Gregg*

Preheat the oven to 200°C, 180°C fan (400°F), Gas Mark 6.

Place 4 pieces of baking parchment, each about the size of a dinner plate, on a work surface. Sit 2 fillets of fish on each piece of parchment, drizzle with olive oil, then arrange the fennel, parsley, olives and cherry tomatoes on top or around them. Season with salt and pepper.

Bring the edges of the baking parchment up around the fish and crimp together to seal tightly.

Transfer the parcels to a baking tray and place in the oven for 12 minutes, until cooked. The aroma when you open them is wonderful.

PESCE SPADA CON BURRO AL LIMONE E CAPPERI

SERVES 4

1 tablespoon olive oil
1 garlic clove, grated
4 x 200g (7oz) swordfish
    steaks, 2.5cm (1 inch)
    thick
Lemon wedges, to serve

For the sauce
55g (2oz) butter
3 teaspoons small capers
3 tablespoons lemon juice
3 teaspoons chopped flat
    leaf parsley

Although swordfish sounds exotic, it's available everywhere in Italy and is widely eaten. That's because it's meaty, versatile and easy to prepare. If you have trouble getting hold of it, use tuna steaks instead. *Rina*

Combine the olive oil and garlic in a baking dish and marinate the swordfish for no longer than 10 minutes, turning once or twice.

Heat a griddle pan until hot but not smoking. Place the swordfish on it and griddle for about 3 minutes per side without moving them (they will stick if you do). Be careful when turning the steaks, as they are delicate. When ready, they should have nice chargrilled lines on them and should be cooked through. Remove from the heat and set aside.

To make the sauce, melt the butter in a small saucepan over a low heat. Add the capers and lemon juice and bring to a simmer. Take off the heat, add the parsley and pour over the steaks.

ROAST DUCK BREAST WITH MARSALA SAUCE

PETTO D'ANATRA ARROSTO CON SALSA AL MARSALA

SERVES 4

4 x 175g (6oz) duck breasts
Salt and freshly ground
   black pepper

For the sauce
15g (½oz) butter
2 shallots, finely chopped
1 garlic clove, chopped
1 sprig of thyme, plus extra
   to serve
1 tablespoon flour
125ml (4fl oz)
   Marsala wine
300ml (10fl oz) beef stock

I came up with this recipe one day when I didn't have any of the usual sweet things to go with my duck breast. Marsala is a sweet fortified wine, so I took a chance and it worked perfectly. It creates a sticky sauce that goes really well with duck. *Anna*

Dry the duck breasts with kitchen paper. Using a sharp knife, score the skin, taking care not to cut into the meat. Season both sides of the breasts with salt and pepper.

Place a dry frying pan over a medium heat. When hot, add the duck breasts, skin-side down, and sear for about 8 minutes. (No oil is needed as the duck will release its own fat.) Turn and cook the flesh side for 5 minutes. Transfer to a plate and keep warm.

Meanwhile, melt the butter in the frying pan, then gently fry the shallots for a few minutes, until softened. Add the garlic and thyme and cook for another minute, before adding the flour. Cook, stirring, for a few minutes.

Add the Marsala to deglaze the pan, then pour in the stock and let it bubble over a medium heat until the sauce has reduced by half. Discard the thyme.

Spoon the sauce over the duck breasts, garnish with a fresh thyme sprig and serve straight away.

POLLO CACCIATORE

SERVES 4

40g (1½oz) dried
    porcini mushrooms
425ml (15fl oz) hot water
Olive oil, for frying
6 echalion (banana)
    shallots, roughly
    chopped
4 garlic cloves,
    finely chopped
8 large chicken thighs,
    skin on
300ml (10fl oz) Italian
    red wine
500g (1lb 2oz) chestnut
    mushrooms, sliced
80g (2¾oz) pitted
    black olives
2 tablespoons tomato
    purée
2 x 400g (14oz) cans
    chopped tomatoes,
    whizzed in a blender
300ml (10fl oz)
    chicken stock
2 teaspoons salt
3 sprigs of thyme
Freshly ground
    black pepper

My dad cooked this for me when I was young, and I was always really impatient to eat it. The smell was amazing! I now cook this for my family, and always make sure there's enough for leftovers because they seem to taste extra good. *Anna*

Preheat the oven to 190°C, 170°C fan (375°F), Gas Mark 5.

Put the mushrooms in a bowl, cover with the hot water and leave to soak for 1 hour. Drain, reserving the liquid (it's worth then pouring the reserved liquid through a sieve lined with kitchen paper to get rid of any grit from the mushrooms.)

Put a glug of olive oil into a large non-stick frying pan over a medium heat and fry the shallots until golden brown. Add the soaked mushrooms, stir well and fry for a few minutes. Add the garlic and fry for about 1 minute, until fragrant. Transfer the contents of the pan to a large ovenproof casserole dish with a lid.

Put another glug of olive oil into the empty frying pan and place over a medium heat. Add half the chicken thighs and fry until golden brown, about 5 minutes per side. Transfer to a plate and fry the remaining chicken thighs in the same way. Add them to the plate too.

Pour the wine into the frying pan and stir with a wooden spoon. Bring to a simmer and bubble gently for a few minutes, until the alcohol has evaporated. Set aside.

Add the chestnut mushrooms to the casserole, along with the olives, tomato purée, blended tomatoes, chicken stock, wine reduction and salt. Season with pepper, and stir. Add in the chicken thighs, skin-side up, and tuck the sprigs of thyme around them. Place the lid on and put in the oven for 1½ hours.

Remove the dish and turn the oven up to 220°C, 200°C fan (425°F), Gas Mark 7. Skim any excess oil off the top, and return to the oven without a lid for a further 20 minutes. Rest for 10 minutes, then serve with Polenta with Parmesan (see page 76).

POLLO ARROSTO RIPIENO

SERVES 4

1 x 2kg (4lb 8oz) chicken
1 lemon, cut into 4 wedges
7 garlic cloves
30g (1oz) butter
4 potatoes, cut into
    wedges
3 carrots, roughly chopped
300ml (10fl oz) white
    vermouth
300ml (10fl oz)
    chicken stock
Salt

For the stuffing
Olive oil, for frying
130g (4½oz) smoked
    pancetta cubes
2 onions, roughly chopped
100g (3½oz) dried
    breadcrumbs
1 egg
Handful of flat leaf
    parsley, chopped
Salt

Who doesn't love a roast chicken? Here it is cooked in the traditional Italian way, with lots of garlic, a generous amount of alcohol and a tasty stuffing that's good enough to eat on its own. *Rina*

Preheat the oven to 190°C, 170°C fan (375°F), Gas Mark 5.

First make the stuffing. Put a glug of oil into a frying pan over a medium heat and fry the pancetta cubes until nicely browned. Add the onions and fry for a few minutes, until softened. Transfer the contents of the pan to a bowl and add the breadcrumbs, egg and parsley. Season with salt and give it a good stir.

Fill the neck cavity of the chicken with the stuffing. Put 2 lemon wedges and 2 cloves of garlic inside the main cavity. Smear the butter over the skin and season all over with salt.

Put the chicken into a roasting tin and place the remaining lemon wedges by the legs. Surround the bird with the remaining garlic cloves, potatoes and carrots, then pour in the vermouth and stock. Cover with foil and roast for 2 hours.

Remove the foil and roast for another 15–20 minutes so that the skin becomes crisp and golden brown.

COSCE DI POLLO ARROSTO CON I CARCIOFI

SERVES 4–6

12 chicken thighs, skin on
Olive oil, for frying
150ml (5fl oz) white wine
2 x 400g (14oz) cans
   artichokes, drained

For the marinade
Juice of 1 large lemon
3 garlic cloves, crushed
3 large sprigs of rosemary,
   broken into smaller
   pieces
100ml (3½fl oz) olive oil
1 tablespoon salt

I learned how to make the marinade for this chicken dish by watching my dad prepare it for barbecues. I find it works just as well for chicken cooked in the oven, and it makes me very happy to serve it to my appreciative family. *Anna*

First prepare the marinade. Pour the lemon juice into a large bowl, add the remaining ingredients and mix well.

Make 2 or 3 diagonal slashes in the skin of the chicken thighs, then place them in the marinade. Toss well and set aside for 30 minutes.

Preheat the oven to 210°C, 190°C fan (410°F), Gas Mark 6½.

Put a glug of olive oil into a frying pan over a medium heat and fry the chicken thighs in batches until lightly browned on all sides, about 5 minutes per side. Be careful as they may spit and sizzle. Transfer them to an ovenproof baking dish, skin-side up.

Deglaze the pan with the wine, using a wooden spoon to scrape up all the sticky bits. Pour this liquid over the chicken, then pour in the marinade, including the rosemary sprigs. Scatter the artichokes around the bird. Cover with foil and place in the oven for 45 minutes.

Remove the foil, and turn the oven up to 220°C, 200°C fan (425°F), Gas Mark 7. Roast for a further 10 minutes to make the skin crisp and golden brown.

Serve with warm crusty bread.

CONIGLIO CON OLIVE

SERVES 2

1 rabbit, chopped into
    pieces (ask your butcher
    to do this for you)
Olive oil, for frying
200ml (7fl oz) white wine
2 garlic cloves, grated
1 onion, roughly chopped
Sprig of rosemary
120g (4¼oz) pitted black
    or green olives
Salt and freshly ground
    black pepper

While visiting wine producers on the island of Ischia,
I discovered that they catch and roast rabbits for lunch.
I brought home this recipe, and the whole family loves it.
The meat is lean yet so delicious. *Gregg*

Preheat the oven to 200°C, 180°C fan (400°F), Gas Mark 6.

Season the rabbit with salt and pepper. Put a glug of olive oil
into a large frying pan over a medium-high heat. When hot,
brown the rabbit in 2 batches – this will take about 8 minutes
– then transfer it to an ovenproof dish.

Pour the wine into the empty frying pan set over a moderately
high heat. Add the garlic cloves and cook for a few minutes,
using a wooden spoon to scrape up the sticky bits. Pour this
liquid over the rabbit.

Add the onion, rosemary and olives to the dish, then place
in the oven for 35–40 minutes.

ROMAN ROAST PORK BELLY

PORCHETTA

SERVES 6

2 tablespoons fennel seeds
60g (2¼oz) thyme leaves,
    finely chopped
60g (2¼oz) rosemary
    leaves, finely chopped
60g (2¼oz) sage leaves,
    finely chopped
8 garlic cloves,
    finely chopped
20g (¾oz) coarse salt,
    plus extra for sprinkling
1 teaspoon sugar
1 teaspoon freshly ground
    black pepper
5 tablespoons extra virgin
    olive oil, plus extra
    for drizzling
1 x 5kg (11lb) whole pork
    belly, boned and scored
    at 1cm (½ inch)
    intervals (ask your
    butcher to do this,
    and be sure to keep
    the bones)

The first time I tried this dish I was in Rome with my husband Massimo. It was lunchtime and we were hungry, so we literally followed our noses toward a delicious smell. We eventually tracked it down to a little alley with a queue outside a shop that was cooking fantastic pork. *Rina*

You must start this recipe 24 hours before you want to eat. Heat a small, dry frying pan over a medium heat, then add the fennel seeds and lightly toast them. Be careful, as they can burn very quickly. Transfer to a mortar and pound them into a coarse powder.

Put the fennel powder into a bowl, add the herbs, garlic, salt, sugar, black pepper and 2 tablespoons of the olive oil and mix to a paste.

Lay the pork flat on a work surface, skin-side down. Rub the paste over the meat, taking care not to get it on the skin. Transfer to a roasting tin, skin-side up, cover with clingfilm and place in the refrigerator overnight.

The next day, take the pork out of the refrigerator and let it sit at room temperature for about 2 hours.

Preheat the oven to 220°C, 200°C fan (425°F), Gas Mark 7.

Place the pork on a work surface skin-side down and roll it up from one of the long ends, trying to get a nice even shape. Using butchers' string, tie the joint tightly at 2.5cm (1 inch) intervals along its length. You do not want it to open up while roasting.

Massage the remaining olive oil all over the joint, then rub a generous sprinkling of salt all over the skin. This will ensure you get crunchy crackling.

Grease a large roasting tin with a drizzle of olive oil and arrange the bones in it. Place the joint, seam up, on top of the bones and add just enough water to cover the bottom of the tin. This will keep the pork moist while cooking.

Roast for 15 minutes, then turn it seam-side down and cook for another 15 minutes.

Turn the oven down to 160°C, 140°C fan (325°F), Gas Mark 3 and cover the pork with foil. Roast for 2½–3 hours.

Remove the foil, turn the oven up to 220°C, 200°C fan (425°F), Gas Mark 7 and roast the pork for another 15 minutes, until the skin bubbles and crisps up.

Take the pork out of the oven, wrap loosely with foil and set aside to rest for at least 30 minutes.

Once the roast has rested, remove the butchers' string carefully, as it will be stuck to the skin. Transfer the roast to a serving plate and carve it through the scores in the crackling to get perfectly portioned slices 1cm (½ inch) thick. *Sensazionale!*

SPEZZATINO DI MAIALE

SERVES 4

2 tablespoons olive oil
2 onions, roughly chopped
2 carrots, roughly chopped
2 celery sticks, roughly
    chopped
2 tablespoons tomato
    purée
2 garlic cloves, crushed
1 teaspoon fennel seeds
500g (1lb 2oz) pork neck,
    cut into 2.5cm (1 inch)
    cubes (ask your butcher
    to do this)
300ml (10fl oz) apple juice
300ml (10fl oz) pork stock
2 bay leaves

Gregg loves stews – they're the kind of working-class food he grew up with. Of course, the ones I make have the flavours of Italy, not southeast London. *Anna*

Preheat the oven to 160°C, 140°C fan (325°F), Gas Mark 3.

Place a large flameproof casserole dish over a medium heat, add the olive oil and cook the onions, carrots and celery for about 5 minutes, until softened.

Add the tomato purée and garlic and fry gently for 1–2 minutes. Stir in the fennel seeds and cook for 1 minute.

Place a dry frying pan over a medium heat. When hot, fry the pork cubes in small batches until browned on all sides. Add them to the casserole dish.

Pour in the apple juice and use a wooden spoon to scrape up all the sticky bits in the bottom of the pan. Tip this mixture into the casserole, add the stock and stir well. Push the bay leaves under the liquid, then cover the dish and place in the oven for 2 hours, until the pork is juicy and tender.

LENTICCHIE CON SALSICCIA

SERVES 2–3

Olive oil, for frying
1 carrot, finely chopped
1 celery stick, finely
  chopped
1 onion, chopped
1 garlic clove, finely
  chopped
6 Italian-style sausages
300ml (10fl oz) stock
2 x 400g (14oz) cans
  lentils, rinsed
  and drained
Salt

I regularly do the shopping when we are in Italy; it's supposed to help me with speaking Italian. I love using little family-run shops – it's such a nice experience, helped by the fact Italians are pretty relaxed about parking in the street. Greengrocers are my favourite, but butchers come a close second – they always have fantastic sausages. *Gregg*

Put a glug of olive oil into a saucepan over a medium heat and fry the carrot, celery and onion for about 5 minutes, until softened. Add the garlic and cook for another minute.

Place the sausages in the pan and fry until browned all over. Add the stock and lentils, cover the pan with a lid and cook over a low-medium heat for 30 minutes.

POLPETTE IN SALSA DI POMODORO

MAKES 16

Olive oil, for frying
2 shallots, diced
2 eggs
120g (4¼oz) dried
    breadcrumbs
Large handful of flat
    leaf parsley, chopped
2 garlic cloves, grated
500g (1lb 2oz)
    minced pork
500g (1lb 2oz)
    minced beef

For the sauce
2 tablespoons olive oil
1 garlic clove
1 onion, chopped
3 tablespoons tomato
    purée
2 x 500g (1lb 2oz)
    cartons passata
1 teaspoon salt
1 teaspoon sugar

This classic recipe allows you to recreate the famous scene from Disney's *Lady and the Tramp* and discover if your husband loves you enough to push his last meatball toward you with his nose. *Anna*

Put a glug of olive oil into a large saucepan over a medium heat and fry the shallots for a few minutes, until softened. Transfer them to a bowl, add the eggs, breadcrumbs, parsley, garlic and minced meats and stir thoroughly with a wooden spoon.

Divide the meat mixture into 16 equal pieces and roll them into balls. This is great fun.

Put another glug of olive oil into the frying pan over a medium heat and fry the meatballs for a few minutes, until browned all over. Transfer them to a plate.

To make the sauce, put the olive oil into a pan over a medium-high heat, add the garlic clove and fry for a few minutes until golden. Be careful it doesn't burn as this will make it bitter. Discard the garlic – you just need the flavoured oil.

Add the onion and fry for a few minutes, until softened.

Lower the heat, squeeze in the tomato purée and fry for 1 minute, stirring to make sure it doesn't catch and burn. Pour in the passata, add the salt and sugar and give it a good stir.

Gently place the meatballs in the sauce, then cook, uncovered, over a low-medium heat for 1½ hours. Serve with spaghetti.

BISTECCA DI OSSA CON MIDOLLO OSSEO

SERVES 4

4 beef marrowbones, each 10cm (4 inches) long
4 x 350g (12oz) T-bone steaks, cut 2.5cm (1 inch) thick
4 tablespoons olive oil
1 garlic clove, crushed
1 teaspoon salt, plus extra for sprinkling
Freshly ground black pepper

A meat-lover's delight, the smell and sizzle of these steaks on a griddle will have you reaching for a knife and fork – and the Chianti bottle. *Anna*

Preheat the oven to 180°C, 160°C fan (350°F), Gas Mark 4.

Place the marrowbones in a roasting tin, sprinkle with salt and pepper and roast for 25–30 minutes.

Meanwhile, remove the steaks from the refrigerator and allow them to come up to room temperature.

Place the oil, garlic and salt in a bowl and mix to combine. Massage this mixture into the steaks and set aside for 1 hour.

Place a griddle pan over a high heat until smoking hot. Add the steaks and cook for 3 minutes per side if you like them medium rare, or 6 minutes per side if you prefer them well done. Transfer to a warm plate, cover with foil and set aside to rest for 8 minutes.

Scoop the marrow out of the bones, spoon it over the steaks and enjoy!

FEGATO DI VITELLI

SERVES 4

2 tablespoons flour
4 x 225g (8oz) slices
   of calves' liver
30g (1oz) butter
2 onions, chopped
15g (½oz) caster sugar
40g (1½oz) raisins
4 tablespoons white
   wine vinegar
Salt and freshly ground
   black pepper

This is such a classic dish that I can't remember when it came into my life. It can be cooked and on the plate in just a couple of minutes – beautifully simple. *Rina*

Put the flour onto a plate and coat the liver in it, shaking off any excess.

Melt the butter in a large frying pan over a low heat, then fry the onions until soft. Stir in the sugar and raisins, then add the liver and fry gently until cooked to your liking – for about 8 minutes if you like it slightly pink in the middle, 10 minutes if you like it more cooked.

Pour in the vinegar and season with salt and pepper to taste. Serve straight away.

COSTINE DI MANZO BRASATE

SERVES 4

Sunflower oil, for frying
2.2kg (4lb 8oz) beef
   short ribs
2 onions, chopped
2 carrots, chopped
2 celery sticks, chopped
2 garlic cloves, grated
2 tablespoons tomato
   purée
125ml (4fl oz) red wine
300ml (10fl oz) beef stock
celery leaves, to garnish

On one of our trips to Italy, Anna and I went to explore the lovely little town of Sarzano in the northwestern region of Liguria. We stopped for coffee and cake on a piazza, but ended up buying some beautiful-looking beef ribs from the window of a butcher's shop. *Gregg*

Preheat the oven to 160°C, 140°C fan (325°F), Gas Mark 3.

Put a glug of sunflower oil into a wide flameproof casserole dish on a high heat. Add the ribs in batches and brown them on all sides, about 10 minutes per batch. Transfer them to a plate.

Add the onions, carrots, celery and garlic to the pan and cook for about 5 minutes, until they begin to soften.

Stir in the tomato purée and wine and heat to allow the alcohol to burn off – about 5–10 minutes. Pour in the stock, give it a stir, then return the ribs to the pan. Cover and cook in the oven for about 3 hours, until the meat is tender. Garnish with celery leaves and serve with Polenta with Parmesan (see page 76).

BRACIOLE

SERVES 4

4 slices of braising steak,
  about 85g (3oz) each
4 slices of Parma ham
3 tablespoons extra
  virgin olive oil
1 quantity Tomato Sauce
  (see page 87)
Salt and freshly ground
  black pepper
Basil leaves, to garnish

For the filling
150g (5½oz) white
  breadcrumbs
4 tablespoons grated
  Parmesan cheese
1 garlic clove, grated
3 tablespoons pine
  nuts, toasted
3 tablespoons freshly
  chopped flat leaf
  parsley
2 eggs, beaten

My mother would get up really early to prepare this, so I would wake up to the aroma of the beef being braised. It would make me very happy and excited because I thought the beef rolls she made with it were the best thing ever! *Rina*

First make the filling. Place all the ingredients for it in a large bowl and mix well. Set aside.

Place the steaks between 2 sheets of clingfilm and beat them lightly with the flat side of a meat tenderizer or a heavy-based saucepan. Don't overbeat or the steaks will tear. Remove the clingfilm and season the steaks with salt and pepper.

Cover each steak with a slice of Parma ham and spread a heaped tablespoon of the filling on top.

To roll the beef, fold the 2 longest sides of each slice into the centre. Then, starting at the shortest end, roll the meat into a tight sausage shape. Secure the rolls with cocktail sticks, or tie them with butchers' string. Don't worry too much about presentation.

Put the olive oil into a pan large enough to eventually hold all your beef rolls and tomato sauce. Place over a medium heat and fry the rolls for a couple of minutes, until golden brown all over. Pour in the tomato sauce, cover with a lid and cook at a gentle simmer for 2 hours. Keep an eye on the pan and if it becomes too dry, add a little bit of water.

Once cooked, set aside to cool slightly, then remove the cocktail sticks or string.

Tear the basil leaves over the dish and serve with a green salad, or with pasta if you feel like having a feast.

BRAISED VEAL SHANKS

OSSO BUCCO

SERVES 4

4 x 500g (1lb 2oz)
   veal shanks
Plain flour, for dusting
50g (1¾oz) butter
2 tablespoons olive oil
1 large onion, finely
   chopped
1 large carrot,
   finely chopped
1 large celery stick,
   finely chopped
1 garlic clove, chopped
2 tablespoons tomato
   purée
250ml (9fl oz) white wine
750ml (27fl oz) chicken
   stock
Salt and freshly ground
   black pepper

For the gremolata
3 tablespoons finely
   chopped flat leaf
   parsley
1 garlic clove, crushed
Finely grated zest of
   1 unwaxed lemon
Pinch of salt

Slow-cooked veal in white wine and tomato sauce is an
Italian classic, and makes a wonderful Sunday lunch.
It's melt-in-the-mouth tender. *Anna*

Dry the veal shanks with kitchen paper, then dust them
lightly with flour – this will help them to brown nicely.

Melt the butter in a large flameproof casserole dish over
a medium heat. Add the shanks and cook until browned
all over. Transfer to a plate and keep warm.

Add the onion, carrot, celery and garlic to the pan and cook,
stirring, for about 5 minutes, until softened. Add the tomato
purée, then return the shanks to the pan. Pour in the wine
and allow it to evaporate over a medium heat for about
5 minutes. Season with salt and pepper.

Pour in 480ml (17fl oz) of the chicken stock and bring to
the boil. Cover the pan and simmer for about 1½ hours, or
until the meat is falling off the bone. Check every 15 minutes,
turning the shanks and adding more chicken stock as necessary.
The cooking liquid should always be about three-quarters
of the way up the shanks.

To make the gremolata, put all the ingredients for it in a
small bowl and mix well.

Sprinkle the gremolata over the veal just before serving.

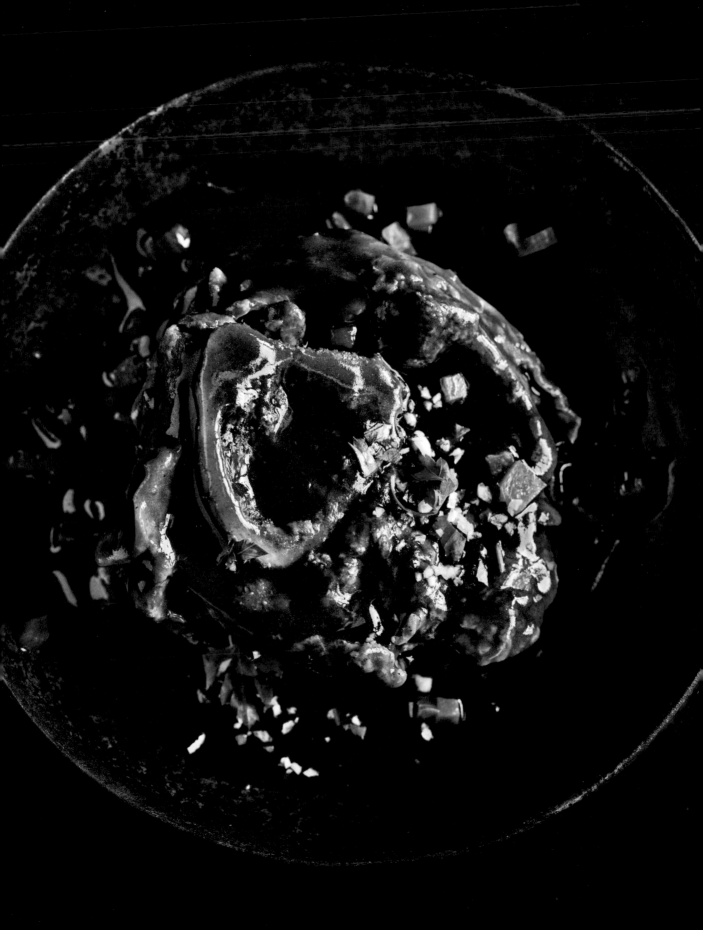

VEAL CHOPS

COSTOLETTE DI VITELLO

SERVES 4

4 tablespoons olive oil
2 garlic cloves, grated
½ tablespoon finely
  chopped thyme leaves
½ tablespoon finely
  chopped sage leaves
½ tablespoon finely
  chopped rosemary
  leaves
1 teaspoon salt
Freshly ground
  black pepper
4 x 325g (11½oz) veal
  chops, each 2.5cm
  (1 inch) thick

During the summer, it's my husband Massimo's responsibility to man the barbecue because he's a real expert. His timing and touch are perfect, so follow this recipe to have great chops just like his. *Rina*

―――――――――――――――――――――――――――

Put the olive oil into a small bowl, add the garlic, chopped herbs, salt and a twist of pepper and stir well. Rub this mixture onto your chops and place them in the refrigerator for 1 hour.

Heat a griddle pan until very hot, then cook the chops on it for 6 minutes per side. Serve with a salad.

COSTOLETTE DI AGNELLO CON SALSA VERDE

SERVES 4

12 lamb cutlets
Olive oil, for rubbing
Salt and freshly ground
  black pepper

For the salsa verde
50g (1¾oz) flat leaf
  parsley, roughly
  chopped
50g (1¾oz) mint,
  roughly chopped
4 tablespoons roughly
  chopped capers
12 anchovy fillets in
  oil, drained and
  roughly chopped
2 garlic cloves,
  roughly chopped
1 teaspoon Dijon mustard
2 tablespoons red
  wine vinegar
250ml (9fl oz) extra
  virgin olive oil
½ teaspoon salt

This is a family favourite that we tend to cook inside, then take outside to eat in the garden. The smell of fresh mint, parsley and tender lamb is divine, and Gregg (who is a massive fan of lamb) can't keep away from these cutlets. *Anna*

First make the salsa verde. Put all the ingredients for it into a blender and blitz for about 40 seconds if you like it chunky, or keep blitzing if you prefer it smooth. Set aside.

Remove the lamb cutlets from the refrigerator and set aside for 30 minutes to bring them up to room temperature.

Place a griddle pan over a medium-high heat. Rub the oil onto the cutlets and season with salt and pepper. Griddle for 2–3 minutes on each side if you like them slightly pink in the middle. Set aside on a warm plate and leave to rest for 5 minutes.

Serve the cutlets with a generous amount of salsa verde spooned over them. *Molto buono*!

VEAL WRAPPED IN PARMA HAM

SALTIMBOCCA

SERVES 4

8 veal escalopes
    (you can use chicken
    or turkey if you prefer)
16 slices of Parma ham
8 sage leaves
30g (1oz) butter
2 tablespoons
    sunflower oil
½ glass (75ml/2½fl oz)
    white wine

Saltimbocca means "jump in the mouth", a reference to how good this dish is. I enjoy seeing Anna jumping around in the garden to pick the sage. *Gregg*

Sandwich each escalope between 2 slices of Parma ham and place a sage leaf on each one. Pin all the layers of each "sandwich" together with a cocktail stick.

Put the butter and oil into a frying pan over a medium-high heat. When the butter has melted, fry the meat gently on each side for 5 minutes, until the ham is crisp. At this point, sprinkle the wine over the meat and let it bubble over a low heat until this meat is cooked and the sauce thickens – about 5 minutes.

Serve with a salad and some crisp roast potatoes.

ROAST LEG OF LAMB WITH ANCHOVIES

COSCIA D'AGNELLO ARROSTO CON ACCIUGHE

SERVES 4

Sunflower oil, for frying
1 x 2kg (4lb 8oz) leg
   of lamb
1 x 50g (1¾oz) can
   anchovies in oil, drained
   and roughly chopped
2 tablespoons olive oil
3 carrots, roughly chopped
6 shallots, cut in half
   lengthways
3 sprigs of rosemary
6 garlic cloves, lightly
   crushed but kept whole
300ml (10fl oz) white wine
Salt

You might think that lamb and anchovies is a strange marriage. Won't the meat taste fishy? The answer is no. The anchovies simply add a savoury depth of flavour. Try it and see! *Anna*

Preheat the oven to 200°C, 180°C fan (400°F), Gas Mark 6.

Put a glug of sunflower oil into a frying pan large enough to hold the lamb. When hot, sear the lamb on all sides until nice and brown – about 5 minutes. Transfer to a roasting tin.

Using a sharp knife, make small incisions all over the lamb and insert the anchovies. Rub the olive oil all over the joint and season with salt. Surround the lamb with the carrots, shallots, rosemary and garlic, then pour in the wine.

Roast the lamb for about 1¼ hours if you like it pink inside, or 1½ hours if you prefer it well done.

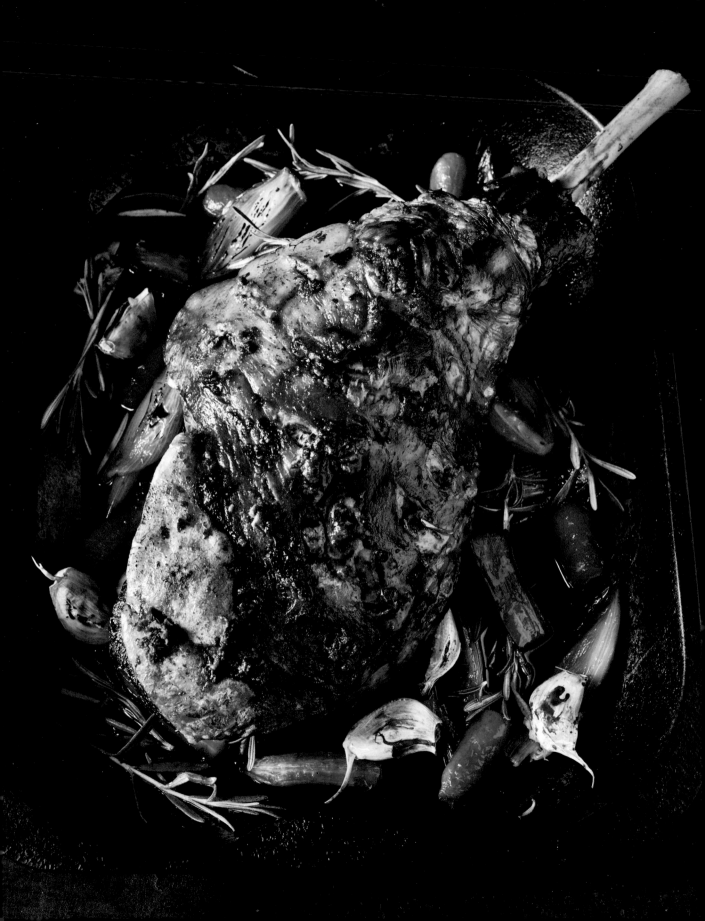

Chapter Four

DESSERTS

ICE CREAM WITH COFFEE

AFFOGATO

SERVES 4

4 scoops good-quality
  vanilla ice cream
200ml (7fl oz) hot strong
  espresso coffee

This is my go-to dessert whenever I'm in an Italian
restaurant. The contrast between cold ice cream and
hot coffee is stunning, a perfect example of delicious
Italian simplicity. *Gregg*

Put a scoop of the ice cream into 4 small dessert bowls.
Pour the hot coffee over the top and tuck in. It's really
as easy as that.

BUDINO AL CARAMELLO

SERVES 6

120g (4¼oz) dark
   brown sugar
½ teaspoon salt
5 tablespoons water
380ml (12½fl oz)
   double cream
190ml (6¾fl oz) milk
1 large egg plus 2 large
   egg yolks
2 tablespoons cornflour
2 tablespoons unsalted
   butter
1 tablespoon rum or
   dark liqueur of your
   choice (optional)

For the caramel sauce
120g (4¼oz) unsalted
   butter
225g (8oz) dark
   brown sugar
165ml (5½fl oz)
   double cream
1 teaspoon vanilla
   extract
Pinch of salt

I make these puddings for Gregg as a treat. I just hope you eat yours a little more elegantly than he does. I'm sometimes tempted to give him a shovel. *Anna*

Put the sugar, salt and water in a heavy-based pan over a medium heat and warm, stirring constantly until a very dark caramel forms. This should take 8 minutes.

Pour in the cream, whisking as you go, then add the milk in the same way. Increase the heat and bring this mixture up to the boil, then set the pan aside.

Place the eggs and egg yolks in a large bowl, add the cornflour and whisk well. Gently pour in the caramel, stirring as you go. Return the mixture to the saucepan and place over a low heat for a couple of minutes, whisking constantly, until thickened. Take the pan off the heat and whisk in the butter. Add the rum or liqueur (if using).

Pour the caramel pudding into glasses, cover with clingfilm and place in the refrigerator overnight to set.

To make the sauce, melt the butter in a saucepan over a medium-low heat. Add the sugar and stir for 2 minutes. Pour in the cream and stir for another 2 minutes.

Take the pan off the heat and stir in the vanilla and salt. Pour the hot caramel sauce into a jug and allow to cool completely.

When your puddings have set, pour a thin layer of caramel sauce over them and serve.

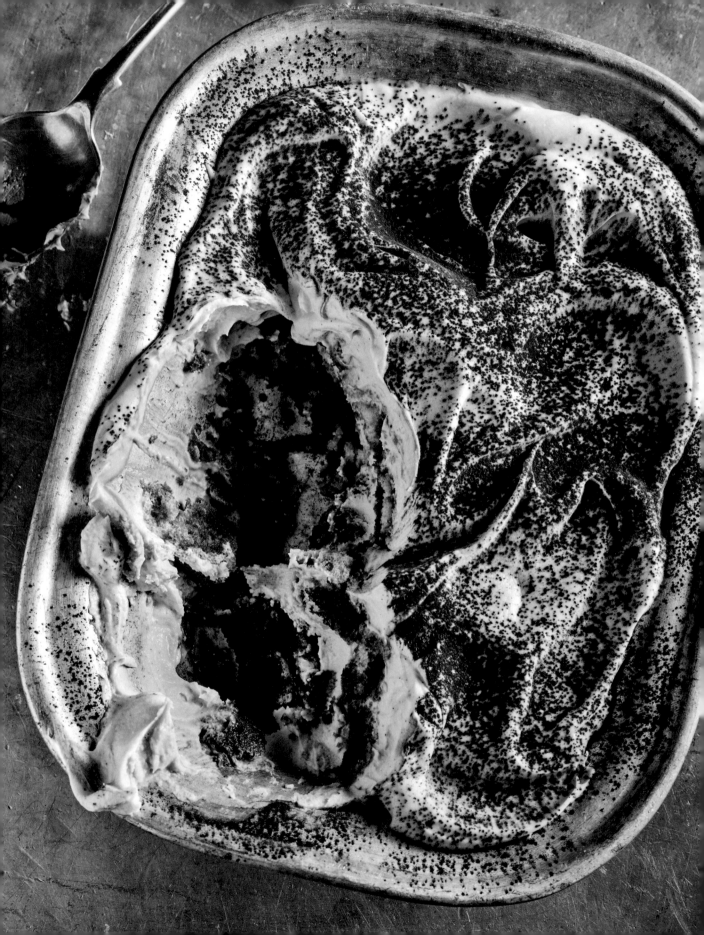

TIRAMISU

SERVES 4

500g (1lb 2oz) mascarpone
    cream cheese
600ml (20fl oz) double
    cream
300ml (10fl oz) Marsala
    wine
1 teaspoon vanilla paste
3 tablespoons icing sugar
425ml (15fl oz) strong
    espresso coffee
2 x 200g (7oz) packets
    sponge fingers
3 tablespoons cocoa
    powder

Traditional tiramisu contains raw eggs, but I avoid them in my recipe below. The dessert is made with sponge fingers soaked in coffee and Marsala that are layered with rich and airy mascarpone cream. Very yummy! *Anna*

Put the mascarpone into a large bowl with the cream, Marsala, vanilla paste and icing sugar and whisk until thick.

Pour the coffee into a shallow dish and dip the sponge fingers in it a few at a time, until soaked but not soggy. Arrange some of the fingers in a 26 x 20cm (10½ x 8 inch) serving dish, just enough to cover the bottom. Spread about one-third of the cream mixture over the sponges. Continue layering until you have used up all the sponges and cream, finishing with a layer of cream.

Dust the top with the cocoa powder, then place the dessert in the refrigerator overnight, or for at least 2 hours.

GELATO AL PISTACCHIO

SERVES 6

140g (5oz) unsalted
shelled pistachio nuts,
plus extra for sprinkling
6 tablespoons milk
1 x 400g (14oz) can
sweetened condensed
milk
1 teaspoon almond extract
300ml (10fl oz) double
cream
80g (2¾oz) dark or
white chocolate chips

In any Italian town at any time of year you can see families and couples strolling out to get a gelato. I'm happy to eat it at any time too, and pistachio is one of my favourite flavours. This recipe is super easy and doesn't need an ice cream machine. *Anna*

Drop the pistachios into a pan of boiling water and cook for a couple of minutes. Drain and allow to cool, then slip the skins off to reveal the bright green colour of the pistachios.

Place half the pistachios in a food processor, add the milk and process to a creamy paste. Add a little more milk if necessary to get the right consistency.

Place the condensed milk and almond extract in a large bowl and whisk until smooth.

In another bowl, whip the cream until it forms stiff peaks. Add this to the condensed milk mixture and whisk for 1 minute. Now add the pistachio paste, chocolate chips and remaining pistachios and stir well. It will look and smell so good that you will be tempted to eat it there and then.

Pour the pistachio mixture into a lidded plastic container and freeze overnight.

Transfer the ice cream to the refrigerator 20 minutes before serving, to allow to soften slightly. Serve sprinkled with pistachios.

SORBETTO ALLA CILIEGIA ASPRO

SERVES 6

550g (1lb 4oz) pitted
    cherries
Juice of 2 lemons
190g (6½oz) caster sugar
125ml (4fl oz) water

Sorbet is always refreshing, but the slightly sour flavour in this recipe is an added bonus. You can add more lemon juice if you want it really sour. *Anna*

Put the cherries into a pan over a medium heat, add the lemon juice, sugar and water and simmer for 5 minutes, stirring constantly until the sugar has melted and the cherries are softening.

Transfer to a blender and blitz to a smooth purée. Strain the mixture through a fine sieve, pressing on the solids to extract as much liquid as possible.

Transfer to a lidded plastic container and place in the freezer overnight.

Transfer the sorbet to the refrigerator 20 minutes before serving, to allow to soften slightly.

GRANITA A LIMONE

SERVES 4

400g (14oz) caster sugar
1.2 litres (40fl oz) water
Juice of 12 lemons
   (about 350ml/12fl oz)
Zest of 2 unwaxed lemons

Come on, you can do this! Granita is really easy to make, yet has incredible texture and flavour. *Gregg*

_____

Place the sugar and water in a saucepan over a medium heat, stirring until the sugar has dissolved. Allow the syrup to bubble and reduce for about 12 minutes, then leave to cool.

Stir the lemon juice and zest into the syrup. If you would like, strain the syrup through a sieve to remove any bits of lemon.

Transfer to a large lidded plastic container and place in the freezer for 1 hour.

Remove the semi-frozen granita from the freezer and mash with a fork so that it looks like crushed ice. Return to the freezer for another hour, then mash again. You will need to repeat the freezing and mashing another 3 times to achieve the correct granita texture.

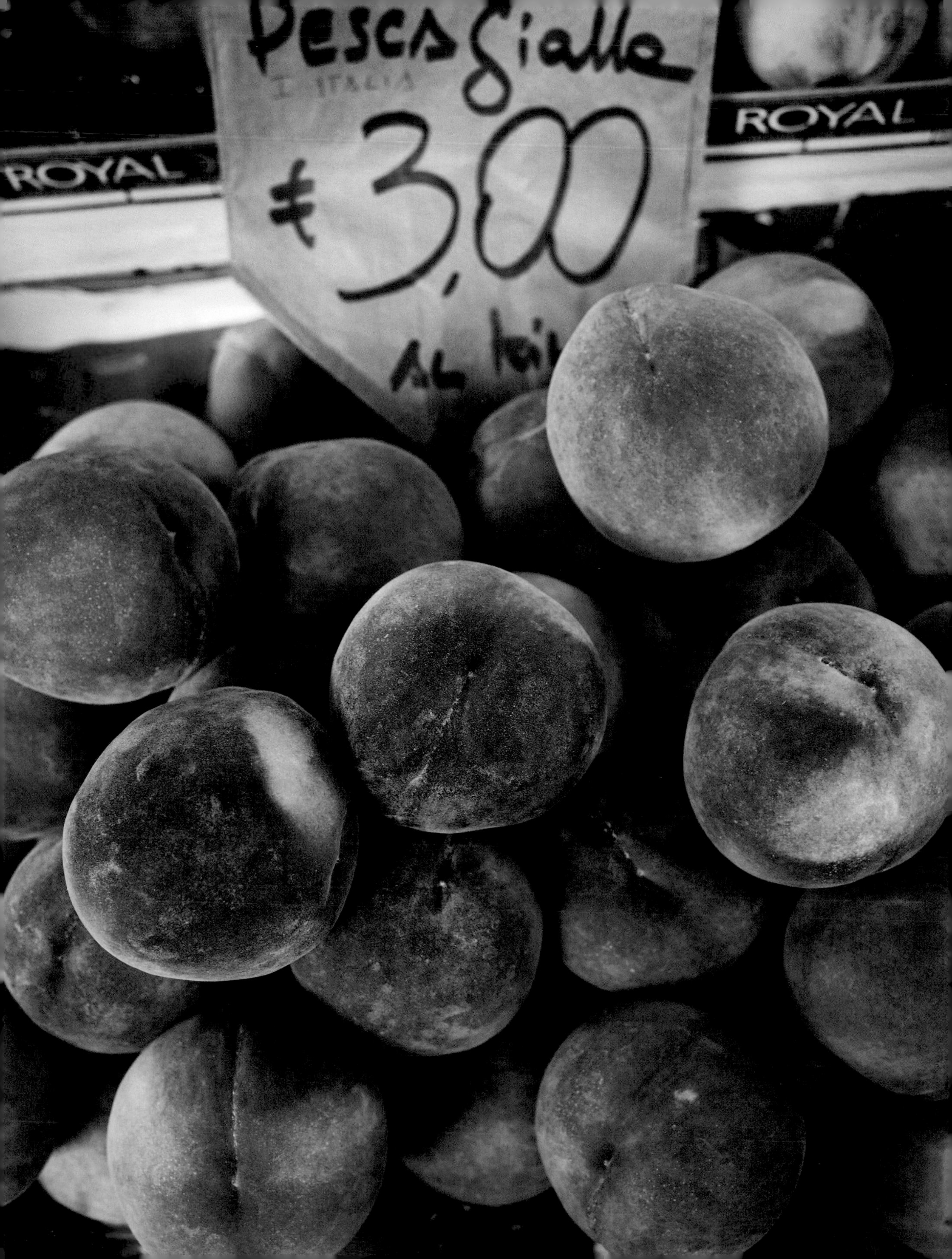
Pesca gialla
€ 3,00
ROYAL
ROYAL

PESCHE ALLA GRIGLIA CON PANNA MONTATA

SERVES 4

200g (7oz) mascarpone cream cheese
2 teaspoons vanilla paste
4 large ripe but firm peaches, halved and stones removed
2 tablespoons melted butter
8 amaretti biscuits, crushed

With their sweet flavour and floral aroma, peaches are delicious just as they are, but grilling them adds to their intensity. The crunch of amaretti biscuits and the smoothness of vanilla cream provide lovely contrasts to the luscious fruit. *Anna*

Put the mascarpone and vanilla paste into a bowl and mix until smooth. Place in the refrigerator.

Place a griddle pan over a high heat. Meanwhile, brush the cut side of the peaches with the melted butter.

When the pan is hot, place the peaches on it, cut-side down, and griddle for 3 minutes. They are ready when the flesh is golden brown and chargrilled lines have formed.

Transfer the peaches to a serving plate. Place a spoonful of the chillled cream in the middle of each half. Sprinkle with the amaretti and serve straight away.

BISCOTTI ALLE MANDORLE

SERVES 4

250g (9oz) plain flour,
   plus extra for dusting
1 teaspoon baking powder
175g (6oz) caster sugar
2 eggs
1½ teaspoons honey
1 teaspoon orange zest
½ teaspoon almond
   extract
130g (4½oz) whole
   almonds

Sweet and satisfyingly crunchy, biscotti are great for dunking in your morning coffee, but are equally good for dipping into a sweet dessert wine, such as Vin Santo. *Anna*

Preheat the oven to 200ºC, 180ºC fan (400ºF), Gas Mark 6. Line a baking sheet with baking parchment.

Place the flour, baking powder and sugar in a bowl. Add the eggs, honey, orange zest and almond extract and mix well until the mixture is soft and crumbly. Using your hands, work in the almonds, then form the dough into a ball.

Transfer the dough to a lightly floured work surface and cut into 2 equal pieces. Roll each piece into a log about 30cm (12 inches) long and 5cm (2 inches) wide. Place them on the prepared sheet and bake for 30 minutes, until golden brown. Set aside to cool for 8–10 minutes before the next step.

Place the logs on a chopping board and use a sharp serrated knife to cut them into diagonal slices about 15mm (⅝ inch) thick.

Lay the biscuits flat on the baking sheet and bake for another 10–12 minutes, until golden brown. Place on a wire rack to cool.

ZEPPOLE

SERVES 4

120g (4¼oz) butter
4 tablespoons
  granulated sugar
Pinch of salt
240ml (8½fl oz) water
120g (4¼oz) plain flour
4 eggs
Sunflower oil,
  for deep-frying
3 tablespoons
  caster sugar
1 teaspoon ground
  cinnamon

Crisp on the outside, soft and fluffy on the inside, zeppole are such a treat – I always had to have one when I went to food markets with my nonna. I still remember holding the warm brown paper bag with greasy fingers and getting sugar everywhere. *Anna*

Put the butter, granulated sugar, salt and water into a saucepan over a lowish heat and stir with a wooden spoon until the butter melts.

Add the flour all at once and beat hard until a soft dough forms. Keep it over a low heat for a couple of minutes, continuing to stir, then set aside to cool for 5 minutes.

Transfer the dough to a bowl and use an electric hand mixer to work in the eggs one at a time, until fully incorporated.

Half-fill a large saucepan with oil and heat until it reaches 190°C (375°F), or a cube of bread added to the oil browns in 40 seconds. Meanwhile, line a plate with kitchen paper.

Use an ice cream scoop to form small balls of dough. Gently add each ball to the pan. Be careful not to splash hot oil on yourself and don't overload the pan: 3–4 balls at a time is enough.

Fry the doughnuts for about 5 minutes, turning over the ones that don't turn themselves. Using a slotted spoon, transfer them to the prepared plate.

When you've finished frying, mix the caster sugar with the cinnamon and sprinkle the mixture over the doughnuts. Eat while still warm.

CANNOLI

MAKES 14

250g (9oz) flour, plus
   extra for dusting
1 tablespoon cocoa powder
30g (1oz) icing sugar
1 teaspoon ground
   cinnamon
1 teaspoon coffee powder
50g (1¾oz) lard
   (vegetable or sunflower
   oil may be used as an
   alternative)
1 egg
2 tablespoons white
   wine vinegar
2 tablespoons
   Marsala wine
1 egg white, for brushing
Sunflower oil,
   for deep-frying

For the filling
2 x 250g (9oz) tubs
   ricotta cheese
40g (1½oz) icing sugar
60g (2¼oz) glacé cherries,
   finely chopped
3 tablespoons chopped
   candied peel

To decorate
14 glacé cherries
Icing sugar, for dusting

The thought of cannoli brings back childhood memories of the *pasticceria* near my Nonna's home. Rows and rows of these delicious sweet treats were displayed in the window and always made my mouth water. *Anna*

Put the flour into a large bowl and add the cocoa powder, icing sugar, cinnamon and coffee. Stir to combine.

Add the lard, egg, vinegar and Marsala and mix well until a dough starts to form. Transfer to a lightly floured surface. Knead with your hands for 5 minutes, until the dough is soft and smooth. Wrap in clingfilm and refrigerate for 1 hour.

Transfer the dough to a lightly floured work surface and use a rolling pin to roll it into a long rectangle about 2mm (1/16 inch) thick. Use a 7.5cm (3 inch) cookie cutter to make 14 circles.

It's usual to shape the cannoli by wrapping the dough around metal tubes about 2.5cm (1 inch) in diameter. Simply roll each dough circle around a cannoli mould and stick the overlapping ends together by brushing them with egg white.

Half-fill a large saucepan with oil and heat until it reaches 180°C (350°F), or a cube of bread added to the oil browns within 1 minute. Meanwhile, line a large plate with a double layer of kitchen paper.

Carefully fry 2 cannoli at a time, turning them often, until golden brown. Using a slotted spoon, transfer them to the prepared plate to drain. Allow to cool completely before removing the moulds.

To make the filling, place the ricotta in a bowl, add the sugar and mix well. Stir in the glacé cherries and candied peel.

Spoon the filling into the cooled cannoli shells. Place a glacé cherry at one end of each cannoli and dust with icing sugar. Enjoy with a cup of coffee.

TORTA AL CIOCCOLATO DI CAPRESE

SERVES 10–12

225g (8oz) unsalted butter, plus extra for greasing
220g (7oz) dark cooking chocolate, plus extra to serve
4 large eggs, separated
180g (6¼oz) caster sugar
Pinch of salt
260g (9½oz) almond flour
cocoa powder, for dusting

This beautiful tart originates from the island of Capri, one of my favourite places in the world. It contains chocolate, and almond flour rather than plain flour, so is very rich and decadent, something I am attempting to be. *Gregg*

Preheat the oven to 190°C, 170°C fan (375°F), Gas Mark 5. Line the bottom of a 20cm (8 inch) springform cake tin with baking parchment and grease the sides with butter.

Sit a heatproof bowl over a pan of simmering water, making sure the bottom of the bowl does not actually touch the water. Place the butter and chocolate in the bowl and stir with a wooden spoon until they melt together. Don't be tempted to turn up the heat or the chocolate will become grainy. Set aside to cool slightly.

Put the egg whites and a tablespoon of the caster sugar into a bowl and whisk into stiff peaks.

Put the egg yolks and the remaining caster sugar into a separate bowl and whisk until thick, creamy and peach-coloured. Add the salt, almond flour and the cooled chocolate and give it a good mix.

Gently fold the beaten egg whites into the chocolate mixture until the bits of white disappear. Be careful as you want to keep it as airy as possible.

Pour the batter into the prepared cake tin and bake in the centre of the oven for 45–55 minutes, until a skewer inserted into the centre comes out almost clean (it is quite a gooey cake). Set aside to cool for about 15 minutes, then remove from the tin.

Transfer the cake to a plate and serve warm or cold, sprinkled with chunks of dark chocolate and dusted with cocoa powder.

PAN DI SPAGNA

SERVES 10–12

120g (4¼oz) plain flour
¼ teaspoon salt
280g (10oz) caster sugar
8 egg whites, at room
  temperature
½ teaspoon lemon juice
1 teaspoon vanilla paste
Icing sugar, for dusting

Here we have a very light and fluffy sponge cake with no dairy. In fact, it's so full of air that if you pick it up and squish it in your fingers, you can hear it squeaking. *Anna*

Preheat the oven to 180°C, 160°C fan (350°F), Gas Mark 4. Set out a 23cm (9 inch) bundt tin, or a standard cake tin – there's no need to grease it.

Sift the flour, salt and half the caster sugar into a bowl, then repeat the sifting twice more. This will make your cake nice and airy.

Put the egg whites into a large bowl with the lemon juice and vanilla paste and beat until soft peaks form (this can be done by hand or in a mixer set at medium speed). Gradually add the remaining sugar a bit at a time, beating constantly until stiff peaks form. Don't overbeat or the mixture will collapse.

Using a metal spoon, gently fold in the sifted flour a little at a time. Do this quickly and lightly to keep the mixture as airy as possible.

Spoon the batter into the cake tin and bake for 25 minutes, or until a cocktail stick inserted near the centre comes out clean. Set aside to cool in the tin upside down.

Turn the cake onto a plate and dust with icing sugar. You can serve it with anything you like, but I like to keep it simple with a dollop of whipped cream and some berries.

BAKED RICE CAKE

TORTA DI RISO AL FORNO

MAKES 12 SQUARES

4 tablespoons
    Amaretto liqueur
100g (3½oz) sultanas
Butter, for greasing
3 tablespoons ground
    almonds, for dusting
120g (4¼oz) Arborio rice
1 litre (35fl oz) whole milk
2 pieces of unwaxed
    lemon zest
5 eggs
150g (5½oz) caster sugar
100g (3½oz) chopped
    candied peel
100g (3½oz) toasted
    flaked almonds
300ml (10fl oz) extra
    thick cream
Icing sugar, to dust

My mum always made this cake on special occasions; it took a while to make, but was worth it. When I was 14 years old I decided to have a go at making it myself, but it wasn't a patch on Mum's. Over the years I'm glad to say that my cooking skills have improved, and my version of this cake is now very good. *Nonna*

Put the Amaretto into a bowl and soak the sultanas for 1 hour.

Preheat the oven to 180°C, 160°C fan (350°F), Gas Mark 4. Butter a 30 x 20cm (12 x 8 inch) baking dish, then sprinkle with the ground almonds, shaking out any excess.

Put the rice into a large saucepan over a low heat, add the milk and lemon zest and bring to a very gentle simmer. Partially cover with a lid (to allow steam to escape) and cook for 45 minutes, stirring occasionally to prevent it from catching on the bottom. Discard the lemon zest, pour the rice mixture into a large bowl and set aside to cool.

Beat the eggs and caster sugar in a separate bowl until combined. Add the rice mixture. Drain the sultanas and add along with the candied peel, flaked almonds and cream. Stir well.

Pour the rice mixture into the prepared baking dish and bake for 45–50 minutes, or until golden on top and a skewer inserted into the middle comes out clean.

Turn off the oven and leave the cake inside for 5 minutes to dry out a bit more. Set aside to cool completely.

Turn the cake out of the tin. Using a serrated knife, cut it into 12 equal squares. Place them on a large serving plate, dust with icing sugar and enjoy. *Dolcezza*!

PANNA COTTA CON CAFFÈ E LIQUORE ALLA NOCCIOLA

SERVES 4

2½ leaves high-strength (platinum grade) gelatine

125ml (4fl oz) instant espresso coffee granules

125ml (4fl oz) boiling water

1 teaspoon Frangelico hazelnut liqueur

50g (1¾oz) golden caster sugar

375ml (13fl oz) double cream

Pinch of salt

4 squares of hazelnut chocolate, finely chopped

I really love making panna cotta, and the first time I made it for my husband it put a smile on his face that made me very happy. Gregg now wants me to make this special-occasion dessert every time people come round for a meal. *Anna*

Place the gelatine in a small bowl of cold water and leave to soften for about 5 minutes.

Put the coffee granules in a cup, add the boiling water and stir to dissolve. Add the hazelnut liqueur and stir again. Transfer to a pan over a low-medium heat, add the sugar and stir until it has dissolved. Pour in the cream, add the salt and bring almost to the boil – about 5 minutes.

Take the pan off the heat. Squeeze the gelatine dry, then add it to the pan and stir really well until it has dissolved.

Strain the mixture through a sieve set over a jug, then pour it into 4 dariole moulds. Set aside to cool slightly before placing in the refrigerator overnight.

Remove the panna cottas from the moulds by dipping the moulds in hot water and inverting onto plates. Serve each panna cotta sprinkled with the hazelnut chocolate.

TORTA DI RICOTTA

SERVES 10–12

250g (9oz) biscotti
125g (4½oz) unsalted
  butter
225g (8oz) cream cheese
550g (1lb 3oz) ricotta
  cheese, drained
200g (7oz) caster sugar
4 eggs
1½ tablespoons cornflour
2 teaspoons vanilla extract
Zest of ½ unwaxed orange
Zest of ½ unwaxed lemon
icing sugar, for dusting

This recipe is lighter and less sweet than standard cheesecake. I loved cheesecake as a girl, and the big wedges we bought from the bakery were placed on white parchment inside a box that was then beautifully tied with coloured string. The cake tastes as good now as it did then. It can be eaten as soon as it's cooled, but I find it tastes better the day after, when it's fully set. *Anna*

Preheat the oven to 180°C, 160°C fan (350°F), Gas Mark 4. Line the bottom and sides of a 23cm (9 inch) springform cake tin with foil (foil is stronger than baking parchment and stops any water from the water bath getting into the cake).

Place the biscotti in a plastic bag and bash with a rolling pin to break them into crumbs. Transfer to a bowl.

Melt the butter in a saucepan over a low heat. Pour it over the crushed biscotti and mix well.

Using your fingers, press the buttered crumbs into the bottom of the prepared tin, then flatten them further using the base of a glass. Bake for 8–10 minutes, until golden brown. Place the tin on a wire rack to cool completely.

Meanwhile, beat the cream cheese in a bowl with an electric hand mixer until smooth; this should take about 2 minutes. Add the ricotta and sugar and beat until combined and smooth.

Beat in the eggs one at a time. Add the cornflour, vanilla and citrus zest and beat just until incorporated. Pour this mixture over the cooled biscotti base and spread evenly.

Place the cake tin inside a large, deep roasting tin, then pour in enough boiling water to come halfway up the sides of the tin. Bake for 60–70 minutes, or until the sides of the cheesecake are set but the centre is still slightly wobbly.

Transfer the tin to a wire rack and allow to cool completely, then cover with clingfilm and place in the refrigerator for at least 8 hours. Serve with a dusting of icing sugar.

INDEX

GLOSSARY

UK	US
Aubergine	Eggplant
Baking parchment	Parchment paper
Banana shallot	Such as zebrune shallot; can use regular shallots
Biscuit	Cookie
Blitz	Process or blend in a food processor or blender
Beef fillet	Beef tenderloin
Borlotti beans	Cranberry beans
Braising steak	Chuck shoulder, ranch or chuck blade steak
Broad beans	Fava beans
Cannellini beans	Also known as white kidney beans
Caster sugar	Superfine sugar
Chestnut mushrooms	Cremini mushrooms
Clingfilm	Plastic wrap
Chips, polenta/potato	Sticks/fries (as in French fries)
Chopping board	Cutting board
Cocktail stick	Toothpick
Cornflour	Cornstarch
Courgette	Zucchini
Desiree potato	Red gold potato
Double cream	Heavy cream
Escalope	Scallop or cutlet
Fishmonger	Fish dealer
Flaked almonds	Silvered almonds
Glacé cherries	Candied cherries
Griddle	Grill (verb) on a stove or BBQ, ridged grill pan (noun)
Grill	Broiler (noun), broil (verb); also see griddle
Icing sugar	Confectioners' sugar
Jug	Pitcher
Kitchen paper	Paper towels
Knob (of butter)	Pat (of butter)
Lardons	Small strips of fatty meat such as bacon or pancetta
Lasagne sheets	Lasagna noodles
Mince (meat)	Ground (meat)
Parma ham	Prosciutto
Passata	Tomato sauce
Plain flour	All-purpose flour
Polenta	Italian version of cornmeal
Pork neck	Pork shoulder butt or blade
Prawns (king)	Shrimp (jumbo)
Semolina	Semolina flour
Single cream	Light cream
Skewer	For testing a cake, you can use a toothpick
Sponge fingers	Ladyfingers
Spring onion	Scallion
Stalk	Stem
Stone	Pit
Sultanas	Golden raisins
Tea towel	Dish towel
Tomato purée	Tomato paste
Whitebait	Smelt